THE Million-
Dollar
RACE

THE Million-
Dollar
RACE

AN INSIDER'S GUIDE TO
WINNING YOUR DREAM JOB

KIRK HALLOWELL, PH.D.

GREENLEAF
BOOK GROUP PRESS

Published by Greenleaf Book Group Press
Austin, Texas
www.gbgpress.com

Distributed by Greenleaf Book Group LLC

For ordering information or special discounts for bulk purchases, please contact Greenleaf Book Group LLC at PO Box 91869, Austin, TX 78709, 512.891.6100.

Design and composition by Greenleaf Book Group LLC
Cover design by Greenleaf Book Group LLC

Publisher's Cataloging-In-Publication Data
(Prepared by The Donohue Group, Inc.)

Hallowell, Kirk.
   The million-dollar race : an insider's guide to winning your dream job / Kirk Hallowell. -- 1st ed.

   p. : ill. ; cm.

   Issued also as an ebook.
   ISBN: 978-1-60832-400-2

   1. Job hunting. 2. Executives--Recruiting. I. Title. II. Title: Million dollar race

HF5382.7 .H25 2013
650.14   2012942964

Part of the Tree Neutral® program, which offsets the number of trees consumed in the production and printing of this book by taking proactive steps, such as planting trees in direct proportion to the number of trees used: www.treeneutral.com

TreeNeutral™

Printed in the United States of America on acid-free paper

12 13 14 15 16 17   10 9 8 7 6 5 4 3 2 1

First Edition

Contents

Introduction

Finding and landing a management position in today's job market is a significant challenge. The consistent change in organizational structures driven by the economy, mergers, acquisitions, globalization, and information technology have resulted in fundamental change in the way organizations find and select top candidates.

It is essential for job candidates who are entering this competitive job market to understand and react to this new level of complexity quickly and effectively. Wonderfully qualified and capable people fail in the job-selection process simply because they are not adequately prepared or do not understand basic dynamics and new rules of job competition.

A few years ago, an individual who focused primarily on their résumé and interview skills could hope to be prepared for the competition. That is no longer the case. Organizations are becoming increasingly sophisticated in the ways they are sourcing job candidates and in the way in which they select from thousands of candidates who typically apply for a management-level position.

This book was written for you if you seek to land a mid- to senior-level leadership position quickly and successfully. This means a job that fits your needs for income, satisfaction, and career development. Social media and open communication structures in organizations have increased direct access to information about companies and jobs. These changes have also leveled the playing field in access to information to job candidates across the world. These changes also mean that top-paying jobs are attracting thousands of applications.

Based on extensive experience in the design of corporate selection processes, scores of interviews with job candidates and recruiting professionals, coupled with a thorough review of emerging candidate-sourcing technology, this book is designed to help you prepare for the immense challenge of landing a senior management position with a structured and rigorous approach.

GETTING THE MOST OUT OF THIS BOOK

This book is intended to support a job search and selection process that may span an extended period of time. Information in each of the chapters will have more relevance based on your immediate needs and your current phase of the selection process. With that in mind, here are a few strategies to consider in utilizing this resource most effectively:

1. Skim the book from beginning to end and identify topic headings, exercises, and questions that seem most relevant to your situation.
2. Immediately access the Million-Dollar Race website (www. TheMillionDollarRace.com). Here you will find forms, exercises, plans, supporting materials, and updates that will keep you current and disciplined in the selection routine.
3. Integrate the book into your job search and selection preparation activities. A regular discipline of job sourcing and networking activities forms the foundation of a successful race.

4. Review specific sections of the book as you approach the next hurdle in your race for selection and focus on specific activities to prepare you for that event.
5. Actively involve your friends and family in a discussion of this book and your ongoing efforts in your bid for job selection. Their input, support, and participation will make the process more rewarding for you and help them understand and accept the eventual outcomes.

There is no question that the job search and selection process can be a significant and extended challenge for many people. Many professionals looking back on a job transition experience find it to be one of the most challenging and frustrating experiences of their lives.

This can also be a time of significant growth, development, and self-understanding that never would have been achieved had the unique constellation of events, experiences, and emotions not been realized. It is my profound hope that this book not only helps you to land a great job, but also helps you to become a more self-aware, confident, and resilient individual. The competition for a high-paying leadership position in today's job market is fierce. The time, effort, and commitment essential to winning the race for selection are within you.

PART ONE: PREPARATION

Part 1 of this book is devoted to preparation for the remarkable challenge of winning your dream job. As in all competitive endeavors, the outcome of the race is largely determined by the quality and consistency of preparation. The actual race in an Olympic hurdles event takes a matter of seconds. The preparation, commitment, and discipline required to succeed in those seconds requires countless hours over a span of many years.

Unfortunately, sensing the need to take immediate action may lead you to react to the situation with undirected activity before you are adequately prepared. Thanks to the career you have built to this point, you have once-in-a-lifetime opportunities to access and leverage your resources and networks. Utilizing these resources before you are fully prepared may result in a significant lost opportunity.

Take time to read this section of the book carefully. Develop the discipline to implement key exercises and answer critical questions about yourself, your dream job, and your ideal organization. Doing so will pay untold dividends as you set out to win.

CHAPTER ONE
The Perpetual Search for a Job of Your Dreams

Andrea didn't see it coming. Her boss requested a meeting with her on short notice. The ninety-minute afternoon appointment was not unusual. It could have easily been about the upcoming budget cycle or the new ERP system migration. It was not.

As she walked into her boss's office, Andrea caught the distant gaze of the vice president of human resources. "Please, have a seat," her boss said in a dry, even tone. "As you may know, we have been conducting a study on workforce planning with Cooper and Schmidt, and we have been looking for ways in which to improve our work-flows and efficiencies." Andrea instantly knew what was happening. She was struck with fear and disbelief. Of course she knew what was going on. Her staff had been working on salary reports for weeks. She never expected that the reduction in force would start with her.

Andrea froze. Her boss's voice drifted away. The vice president's occasional interjections didn't even register. All Andrea could imagine was what it would be like to be out of a steady job for the first time in twelve years. What would she say to her husband and children? Where should she begin?

Organizations grow. They hire people. Boards and investors demand financial performance. Business conditions change. Mergers and acquisitions take place. Reducing headcount is a knee-jerk reaction that yields an immediate impact on the bottom line. The continuous flow of "workforce optimization"—outsourcing, offshoring, industry consolidation—ensure this cycle will continue regardless of economic conditions.

What this means for the mid- to executive-level manager is that the idea of job security within one, or even a few, companies is a thing of the distant past. With a temporary exception in the 2008 economic downturn, the average tenure for a management position has dropped steadily for decades and there is no indication that this trend will change. Chances are that even the most capable and productive of leaders will encounter a job transition due to changes that are out of their control.

As the competition for top-paying management positions continue, more people have access and are vying for a limited number of positions. The new ecosystem of open access to the job markets has leveled the playing field for both organizations and job candidates. Some of the interesting trends that have emerged for this new environment include:

- Smaller firms are attracting executive talent from Fortune 500 companies, getting a level of experience and sophistication not previously accessible.
- Executives and senior managers are more flexible in compensation expectations and willingness to relocate.
- There is extreme competition for desirable jobs and remarkable access to job candidacy. A typical $120,000-plus per year management position may attract 1,500 to 5,000 applicants in this market.

For organizations, the process of selecting top managers and executives must still be as precise as possible. Organizations need to find the correct balance between overlooking the right candidate because their selection processes are too exclusive and hiring the wrong person because they have not been stringent enough. This demand has led to the development of sophisticated and scientifically based selection processes that are continually evolving.

If you are competing for a senior-level professional, manager, or executive position and plan to hold that position for five years, you are in a race for a million dollars or more in compensation and benefits that you would earn during that time. If search fees, bonus structure, relocation, and comprehensive benefits are included, a position with a salary of $150,000 can actually cost the organization well over $250,000 to fill.

Through the power of job boards and social media, there are thousands of people applying for each of these jobs. Organizations are increasingly sophisticated in the way they source, assess, and select talent. The senior-level job interview is only part of the equation. Organizations, search firms, and consulting practices have implemented consistent, rigorous, and highly effective selection processes that provide the predictive success essential to justify this investment.

In this market, job candidates can expect extensive preemployment screening, psychological and cognitive testing, in-depth access to their employment history with verification through the Internet, immediate access to references, and an extensive series of interviews. Without a clear, disciplined approach for preparation and execution of a competitive job campaign, the chance of you landing a job that fully fits your career and income needs is minimal.

THE OLYMPIC HURDLES

This book is based on the Olympic hurdles race as a metaphor for the intense competition involved in every race to win a top management position. To win, each hurdler must be remarkably fit. The competitor not only has to run quickly but also must coordinate each step and jump each hurdle with precise timing and grace. It's not enough to simply clear the hurdles; the successful runner needs to execute each hurdle in succession with consummate pacing. This book is organized around the preparation and conditioning necessary to prepare for the race, followed by ten specific hurdles that the successful candidate must clear to win the race.

The first part of the book is focused on conditioning, which is absolutely essential to competitive athletes. Hurdlers will invest a hundred hours in practice for every minute in an actual race. Unfortunately, most job seekers jump into the process without proper conditioning. They blast down the track to job selection with poor form, knocking over hurdles and wasting valuable time.

The first half of the book is focused on four critical conditioning routines essential to preparation for the selection race:

1. **Managing fear.** Overcoming fear is the foundation of competitive conditioning. Understand what fear is and how you can systematically overcome fear to be successful.

2. **Defining your ideal job.** One of the most common mistakes that competitors make in running the race for selection is not starting with a clear description of their ideal job. Clarify your career objectives as the basis of deciding which jobs you will choose to purse and the opportunities you will actively avoid.

3. **Defining your ideal organization.** Pursuing job opportunities in organizations that are not a fit for you wastes precious time and energy. Determine what types of organizations will be best suited for you, your style, and your career aspirations.

4. **Assessing yourself.** Throughout the job-selection process your interactions and behaviors will be rigorously and persistently scrutinized. Take stock of yourself, your strengths and weaknesses, especially from the perspective of others.

The second half of the book is represented by the ten hurdles of an Olympic hurdles race, starting with shaping your résumé and by nine additional hurdles that are typically encountered by job candidates. Each chapter focuses on the nature and technical construction of the hurdle from the company's perspective and provides specific strategies for approach and form to enable you to clear the hurdle with grace and accuracy. Each of the hurdles is organized in a logical progression and should be addressed one after another. If a particular hurdle is not relevant to your particular situation, you just have one fewer hurdle to jump.

STARTING POINTS

All successful hurdlers have a clear strategy and a clear vision for winning the race. They know the "big picture" of the competition and what it takes to win. Begin your race with the same foundation by embracing these realities.

Reality One: A Poor Job Fit Is a Failure

Lack of alignment among your ambitions, skills, and experience with the demands of a particular job serves absolutely no one, most importantly, not you, the candidate. This book gives you a structured approach to prepare and deliver the best possible performance in your selection campaign. This is not about playing games with the hiring process or misrepresenting yourself. An unsuccessful hire is not only costly for the company but for you as well. A bad hiring decision could negatively impact your career far more than the challenge of an extended job search.

What you can expect from using the information in this book is that you will be prepared to present the best possible representation of yourself to the hiring organization of your choice. You will be far less likely to make a significant error or to leave a significant gap in your preparation. This serves both you and the hiring company by enabling both parties to make the most accurate assessment and decision possible.

Reality Two: Race Preparation and Execution Is a Full-time Job

This book will provide you with a framework for preparing for the selection process, but it cannot do the work for you. In order to be successful at applying the principles in this book you will need a dedicated time to prepare and execute race strategy every day. This may seem excessive unless you fully consider the consequences of not being fully prepared. This book will suggest the best things to do to use that time efficiently, but without a commitment to the preparation and a disciplined plan to implement, no set of ideas will have significant impact on your success.

Reality Three: Expect Quick Results *and* Prepare for a Long Haul

The race to obtain a high-paying job that directly meets your career objectives can be achieved in as little as a few weeks. It is also not uncommon for an executive to work through a job campaign of twelve to eighteen months. You must prepare quickly for the possibility of an ideal opportunity emerging in the early stages of your search. You must also enter the race with a level of commitment, persistence, and tenacity that will see you through to the finish in a long-term effort. A key opportunity to achieve this level of resilience is to remember that the big race is made up of many smaller races, and every contact, meeting, and interview should be celebrated and appreciated as a necessary stride to the eventual victory.

With these realities in mind, this book will help you to prepare and execute your race for selection in a planned and disciplined
approach. Your immediate need to take action may tempt you to
skip over the thorough preparation activities listed in Part One. As
in the case of any competitive event, the eventual success or failure
of your race is determined by your level of preparation. In fact, experience with job candidates who have become derailed in their job
search invariably points to errors or omissions in their preparation
routine. Make a commitment that you will approach this critical
competition with diligent and thoughtful conditioning.

CHAPTER TWO
Managing Fear

Being out of work can be a frightening experience. You are likely to endure emotionally low points as you transition into being unemployed. You might experience periods of doubt, anger, frustration, and even betrayal when an organization chooses to let you go. This is all normal and healthy. And you have an opportunity to work through this quickly.

The ambiguity, stress, and potential frustration associated with entering the race for a competitive job can take a toll. Fewer things will impact your performance in the selection than the thoughts and feelings you bring to the process. A consistent state of fear will inevitably diminish your performance. All successful athletes recognize that fear is part of the competition, and they develop strategies to manage it.

A positive and relentless mindset is the foundation for any challenging life endeavor. Without addressing the way you think and feel about the race, understanding the mechanics and strategies of the selection process will have relatively little impact.

If you have had a successful career and lost your position due to factors outside of your control (downsizing, merger, acquisition, reorganization, etc.), you may feel nothing but an intense desire to have a job. If you have lost your position due to a perceived mismatch with culture, performance concerns, or poor boss relationship, you may feel deeply vulnerable. This chapter is devoted to actively managing that sense of fear and need.

Recruiters and hiring managers have a distinct interest and appreciation for working with individuals who are currently in jobs. Companies that contract external recruiters or search firms frequently require that a percentage of the candidates presented are currently employed. Justified or not, this line of thinking is driven by the assumption that employed people are more prized than people who are out of work. There may even be a subtle or overt assumption that people who are out of work are in some way responsible for their situation. Your challenge is to overcome these perceptions.

It takes consistent discipline and strength of mind to truly form a winning mindset when reality (e.g., bills and checking account balance) points you in another direction. Just as in preparing for the Olympic hurdles, there are some basic, proven approaches that will build your strength and endurance.

UNDERSTANDING FEAR

Fear is the deepest and darkest of all human emotions. Created by billions of years of natural selection, fear is the basic instinct and drive that has kept each species from slipping into oblivion. It is important to understand fear from its mechanical and biological nature. Without digressing into an entire discourse on brain and endocrine function, understand that the sense of fear and the resulting behaviors driven by fear are deeply rooted in our physical structure.

Our instinctual need to face or retreat from perceived danger—fight, flight, or freeze—is remarkably powerful and consistent.

Rooted in the limbic system of the brain, fear limits our repertoire of responses to perceived threats and often leads us to take actions that immediately reduce risk. The significant challenge for you as you approach the selection race is that you absolutely must overcome these natural reactions to fear to be successful.

The good news is that you have moved through a successful career to this point. You have inevitably faced fearful and stressful situations in the past. The fact that you have persisted and demonstrated success in a competitive arena indicates that you do have the capacity, intellect, and drive to manage fear and overcome adversity. The ability to actively manage fear will help you become a more resilient, vibrant, and resourceful person. This capacity will also make you a strong job candidate.

THE THREE A's OF MANAGING FEAR

Fear is a reaction that is deeply wired into our psyche and our bodies, and it is difficult to deny, fight, or overcome directly. When feeling fearful, a natural response is to rationalize or escape the fear through denial or distraction. A more successful approach is to acknowledge fear for what it is, a healthy, natural, and instinctual response to a situation, and then employ a strategy to move beyond it.

You can become more successful at managing fear if you practice a simple, three-step reconditioning technique every time you become aware that you are experiencing fear. Incorporate this discipline into your daily activities, and you will quickly develop a greater sense of control and well-being in your life:

1. **Awareness:** In many cases fear can be a gnawing, uncomfortable feeling that lingers just below the level of perception. This increases our stress level because we experience the fear reaction without knowing what to do about it. The first step in being able to control the fear is to acknowledge it by simply

saying out loud, "I am feeling fearful. This is a very normal and healthy reaction given the situation I'm in right now." Make it a habit to say this clearly, loudly, and repeatedly.

2. **Acceptance:** This is a very brief but important step, and it is a matter of choice rather than any kind of rationalization. Acceptance simply means making an active choice to accept the situation you are in and that fear is part of that situation. It is also helpful to accept the circumstances that surround the fear. This by no means makes the fear go away. It simply allows you to accept that the fear is real and has an impact, and that acceptance clears the way for you to move on to the final step of reconditioning.

3. **Action:** Any time that you take a planned and thoughtful action that directly challenges your fear, you are, by volition and intent, taking control of the situation. Every action that you complete that challenges the fear, moves the fear control backward and moves you closer to the driver seat. Taking direct action against fear is challenging and, as with any discipline, with practice it can be extremely rewarding and even fun. All successful athletic competitors realize this and use this dynamic challenge to drive their performance.

STRATEGIES FOR MANAGING FEAR

In my experience working through my own fear reactions and the fear reactions of many clients, I've found that the action step of the three A's technique to be the most challenging. Here are some simple strategies that will make taking actions against fear more manageable and successful:

- **Start small and build.** Don't try to overcome a fear of heights by climbing the highest tree you can find. If you have a fear of networking, call an old colleague you haven't talked to in a while, blend in a conversation about your current situation, and ask if they have any ideas or suggestions.
- **Write an action plan.** Nothing could be more helpful than making a list of actions you will take and the dates by which you will accomplish them. Checking off items on the list as you complete them helps you to build a sense of accomplishment and helps you to hold yourself accountable for completing the action in a specific time frame.
- **Build reminders.** Make some simple reminder notes with the words "awareness, acceptance, and action" and post them on your phone, your desktop, the dashboard of your car, or office bulletin board. Each time you read them you will reinforce your implementation of this technique in your daily consciousness and activities.
- **Attack fear with boldness.** Take an occasional bold step. Choose to do one thing that is very uncomfortable or a stretch for you. Act on this quickly and trust your intuition.
- **Celebrate successes.** The road to success is paved with small victories. It is absolutely essential that you acknowledge you successes along the way. Making this a habit will increase your overall success and build your fear tolerance.

Working through your fears on a regular basis is much like physical conditioning. At first the routines may feel awkward and unnatural. As you discipline yourself to routinely attack fear, you will find that the process of thinking through fear and taking meaningful action becomes second nature. As you apply this technique to your job search, you may find the approach reaches expression in other parts of your life as well.

A Brief Illustration

Robert was desperate. After his company was acquired by a large, multinational corporation, Robert knew that his VP-level accounting position would be terminated within the first three months of the transition. He knew it was time to get to work on his résumé, start networking, and begin calling search firms, but he simply couldn't begin the process. Whenever he set aside time to edit his résumé, other, more immediate issues took priority. Days passed, and knowing that he had not made any progress on his impending career transition, Robert was growing increasingly uneasy.

During a conversation with Sheila, a long-time peer and confidant, Robert shared his frustration. Sheila recognized that Robert was having a fear reaction to his situation and the fear was inhibiting him from moving forward. Sheila simply walked Robert through the three A's of managing fear:

1. Awareness: Sheila asked him if he was feeling fearful, and when he admitted that he was, she asked him to describe the feelings. He did so.
2. Acceptance: Sheila asked Robert what specifically about this situation was making him feel fearful and what specific behaviors he was avoiding. Robert took full accountability for his predicament.
3. Action: Sheila asked Robert to find and print a copy of his current résumé. Robert walked back to his desk, printed his résumé, took it back to Sheila's office, and in the final ten minutes of their meeting, the pair made several edits to the career objectives section of the résumé. Robert had taken action, and already he felt less fearful. He planned to continue editing the résumé that evening.

The three A's guided Robert in taking incremental action toward success. As Robert's story illustrates, fear melts in the wake of purposeful action.

APPLYING THE THREE A's TO RACE CONDITIONING

Overcoming fear can be an outstanding ally as you prepare for the race. Fear can motivate you to get out of bed in the morning and focus on the top priorities you need to achieve that day in preparation for the race. Overcome fear by reaching out to a colleague to whom you haven't spoken in years, whom you fear might not be receptive to your call. Call an employee who works for a target company and ask for their perspective on working in that organization. Ask a friend to sit down and practice your interviewing techniques.

Break the circle of fear in the moment by taking a quick break to reflect and plan. This may be as simple as taking a long walk, working out, talking with a good friend, or taking time for quiet meditation. The critical factor is that you approach this diversion as a temporary action, to gain your footing, build a little perspective, and return as quickly and decisively to the awareness, acceptance, and action routine. If an action seems too overwhelming to engage in immediately, simply take a slice of that action that's manageable, one that you can move forward within the current moment.

SAMPLE ACTIONS TO DRIVE AWAY JOB SEARCH FEARS

Table 1.1 lists common fears associated with running the race for selection and sample actions that could mitigate that fear.

The second part of this book breaks down all the specific actions essential for running the race. There will be plenty of time and attention for the specifics of sourcing jobs and creating your platform. We will get to that. For now, focus on the discipline of preempting the fear response by taking hold of the moment and working through the three A's.

Table 1.1: Common Fears and Potential Actions

Common Fear	Potential Action
Thoughts that there are too many competitors with more skills and experience	Write down your top five accomplishments from your last position and how you achieved results.
Worrying about spending and cash flow	Review your checking account and charge card statement and identify ten charges you can eliminate this month.
Wondering about the effectiveness of your interviewing skills	Identify five interview questions and practice with a friend while recording.
Not making enough contacts	Systematically review your e-mail and social networking accounts and connect with every contact that makes sense.
Stressing out about not having more structure in your week	Develop a weekly schedule with very specific times for job search activities.

MANAGING FEAR BY MAINTAINING PERSONAL HEALTH AND WELLNESS

The key to success in entering and winning the selection race is persistence, and persistence is based on your capacity for resilience. Resilience can be defined as the capability to respond effectively or "bounce back" in a stressful situation for a prolonged period of time. An individual's capacity to be resilient is, again, based on mental and physical conditioning. The stronger your mind and body are, the greater capacity you have for resilience.

So what can you do? Again, there are many excellent resources on maintaining physical and emotional health. The challenge is committing to your personal health and wellness as part of your regimen in preparation.

You know the drill:

- **Diet:** Eat regularly and manage sugars, saturated fats, and avoid overeating.
- **Exercise:** Maintain regular and consistent physical activities that increase heart and breathing rate for a prolonged period.
- **Relationships:** Establish and maintain a healthy and meaningful network of supportive interactions with friends, family, and colleagues.
- **Substance moderation:** Either completely avoid or moderate the use of alcohol, nicotine, prescription drugs, and recreational drugs.

We know all these things are beneficial. If you were serious about preparing for a hurdles race, you would study the exact combination of diet and conditioning to maximize your performance. It is equally important to maintain these areas as you prepare for one of the most important races of your life.

BREAKING DOWN FEAR THROUGH PLANNING AND DISCIPLINE

One of the greatest challenges of entering the race for selection is that suddenly you do not have all the structures that typically keep people on schedule and busy. Suddenly the onslaught of e-mail, calls, meetings, and tasks ceases. In the wake you may find the remarkable challenge of discovering what you will do with your days.

The final strategy for managing fear on a long-term basis is developing a regular discipline and plan for preparing for and executing your job search. If you have made a firm commitment to achieve a specific number of goals each day and week, and you regularly follow through on that level of commitment, you'll find that your job search builds a regular flow and intensity over time. This is essentially setting the pace of your race.

Competitors with a disciplined and scheduled approach will achieve their goals. If you get knocked off course by challenges and setbacks, you will always have a regular routine to fall back on. Settling back into a structured approach and plan commits you to action. Moving forward with action will always help you manage fear.

POWER STRATEGIES FOR PLANNING AND DISCIPLINE

You have successfully implemented projects in your work experience. You know that disciplined project management requires scope specifications, timeline, budget, resources, and people requirements. Your job preparation and execution of the race for selection is at the core, simply a project. Keep in mind these strategies for maintaining the discipline and planning:

- **Establish your space.** One of the clear advantages of commuting to work is that there are clear physical boundaries defining your workplace. If you are conducting your job search out of your home, establish a space to use for your search.
- **Establish a block of time.** Many of the activities involved in preparation, including career planning, résumé writing, and planning, require protected blocks of time, typically two or three hours. Determine a block of time that you will devote to your search each day and protect it religiously.
- **Set daily and weekly goals.** It is very easy to get off track with your daily and weekly goals, especially when you start traveling and interviewing. Setting simple to-do lists for your week and day and setting up your calendar for appointments is a great first step in building structure.
- **Build activity tracking.** One of your supports for the long haul is to carefully track your progress. If you are using Outlook, consider using the "task" function to keep an ongoing record of your activities.

- **Build in diversity and breaks.** Your job preparation and search can only take so many hours of the day. Plan frequent breaks, including walks, meditation, exercise, errands, and recreational activities to break up the day.

Additional resources for structuring your disciplined approach to job preparation are available on the Million-Dollar Race website (www.TheMillionDollarRace.com).

Entering the race for the job of your dreams can be an immensely challenging experience. This can be especially true if you have experienced years of relative stability and predictability in a full-time position. The sheer amount of change in terms of increased day-to-day ambiguity and steep learning curve you will encounter may be daunting. As you continue to prepare for your selection process, accept the reality that this is by nature a trying time and even the most seasoned and capable leaders can struggle with the transition.

The most important accomplishment of this phase in the race is that you get grounded with a strong mindset-based clear resolution to do whatever it takes for as long as it takes to achieve your goals. This level of commitment and focus will lead you through the most trying of circumstances and you will land that job. The next step of the race is to clearly define what that job of your dreams looks like so that you can clearly communicate that to the world.

QUESTIONS FOR REFLECTION

In the first preparation step, managing fear, we have reviewed broad areas in which you must be conditioned to move through the remarkably challenging process of job transition. Allowing yourself to be sucked in by the natural feelings of sadness, loss, or frustration will inevitably slow you down as you enter the race. Consider these critical questions as you condition for this intense competition:

- **Awareness:** As you think about the selection process, what are your specific fears? List three to five events that elicit some degree of fear as you think about them.
- **Acceptance:** Recognize that your fears are legitimate and real— simply because you are experiencing them. What action or lack of action on your part helps build these fears?
- **Action:** For each fear, list at least one action and a deadline by which you will accomplish this action. Upon taking action, do you experience a difference in your level of fear?

CHAPTER THREE
Define Your Ideal Job

You are not just looking for a job. You are looking for a career opportunity that will add to your fulfillment and contentment in life. Many people who successfully navigate a job transition wish they had taken the opportunity sooner. They often move on to a better fit of assignments, organizations with greater career opportunities, and a constellation of work activities and a culture that is great fit for them.

It is difficult to find something unless you know exactly what you are looking for. The first step in your conditioning process is to define your ideal job. If you have a remarkable urge to jump right into the job search, resist the temptation. Creating your ideal job definition will achieve three outcomes that can save you countless hours and frustration down the road. Stating your conditioning routine by writing your ideal job description will:

- **Keep you from running down rabbit holes.** There are countless career opportunities and alternatives available to you.

Examining, evaluating, and potentially pursuing each opportunity takes precious time and resources. Focus only on the opportunities that meet your expectations.

- **Provide a solid template by which to evaluate opportunities.** A written document will allow you to quickly evaluate opportunities against key specifications.
- **Begin your sourcing and networking activities with laser focus.** To make the most of your networking activities, you must be able to clearly articulate your interests.

While all these points may seem self-evident, a remarkable number of job candidates skip over this important step. Instead of seeing their job transition as a unique opportunity to review their career path and goals, they rush forward into the job search with little direction or clarification. The results are always lower performance and a higher percentage of poor choices. Investing a few hours into your career clarification may be some of the most productive time you will invest in your race.

Listed next is a three-step procedure to put together an ideal job description. You may find the step-by-step process helpful or you may find it constraining. If the latter is the case, feel free to jump from step to step and use the tools and exercises suggested in your own sequence.

STEP ONE: DEFINE WHAT ENGAGES YOU

The "engagement movement" has taken organizations by storm over the past two decades. Consistent research has shown that employees who are more engaged in their work are more likely to produce higher-quality work, produce greater results, and are less likely to leave an organization for another opportunity. So what is this concept of "engagement" all about?

There are many working definitions of employee engagement and, based on extensive review of the literature, here's my academic definition: "An emotional and cognitive attachment to work that motivates behaviors consistent with the objectives of the organization."

I prefer the definition "Engagement is what jazzes you about your work."

If you can remember a time when you were fully engaged in your work, then you can probably remember the sense of accomplishment, purpose, meaning, and the resulting energy you achieved. You know that while you were in that state, you were producing work that represented your highest potential.

The first step in defining your career focus is to determine what your essential motivations and drives are and what kind of work environment is most likely to engage you. The clearer you are about your motivations and preferences for a work situation, the better you are at articulating your goals and finding the motivation to persist in a race that works for you. A quick way to identify your conditions of engagement is to complete the following three writing exercises:

1. Think about a time you were in a work situation, perhaps early in your career, which you were consistently focused on your work and you felt a sense of joy, meaning, or passion about what you were doing. Describe the exact work situation in terms of the exact behaviors you were taking on and your interaction with your environment (interaction with equipment, technology, people, etc.). Write one or two paragraphs describing the situation.

2. Now think about what in that situation made you clear and energized? What made you feel and think positively about that situation? Was it the quality of interaction you had with others? Was it a sense of accomplishment? Was it a specific outcome or reward that you achieved? Write down in a series of words or brief statements the key conditions under which you experienced engagement in a situation.

3. Now think about your future. As you think about your potential career objectives for the future, what are the key defining attributes of the kind of work and the kind of organization you want to be the target of your career focus? What kind of work do you hope to be doing in two to three years?

If you repeat this set of exercises a few times, describing different situations in which you were fully engaged, you can start to shape some key characteristics of the kind of work and the kind of work setting that will keep you most engaged.

STEP TWO: WRITE YOUR IDEAL JOB DESCRIPTION

Now that you have some indication of the kind of work that you find most engaging, it is time to focus on the ideal position you would like in your next job. Regardless of the trials and tribulations you may have encountered during your job search to date, it is absolutely essential to put away any doubts that you can have the job of your dreams. In fact, people achieve this outcome on a regular basis. Though it may not be as fast or as easy as people would like, it happens consistently.

Without a clear vision of what your dream job looks like in terms of accountability, span of control, company culture, location, salary range, etc., you will subject yourself to looking at countless possibilities with no clear way to narrow your focus.

As a template for this exercise, look at the job listings from some progressive companies that have attracted your attention. Highlight parts of the listing that you find particularly engaging and meaningful. Once you have a collection of highlighted position descriptions, begin drafting the precise statements and accountabilities that most appeal to you. Your output should be a complete job posting for a job that completely fits all your expectations.

Following are some guiding questions, broken down thematically, that will help you write your ideal job description.

Job Requirements

- What are your major day-to-day accountabilities? (List five to seven major accountabilities.)
- What are your major goals or initiatives for your first year on the job?
- Will you have full budget (profit and loss) accountability for your area of the organization?
- What is your ideal reporting structure (total number of direct reports)?
- What is your ideal span of control in terms of total headcount, geography, divisional structure, gross revenues, etc.?
- What key opportunities are you looking for that will stretch you and build your career platform?

Salary and Total Compensation Requirements

- What are your minimum salary requirements?
- Are equity options (stock grants or options) essential for you?
- What is your desired salary, bonus, and/or commission structure?
- Do you need full benefits for yourself? For dependents?
- Are you looking for cross-functional rotations or international assignments?
- What other specific perks or opportunities are you looking for (e.g., continuing education benefits, development assignments, company car, etc.)?

Location and Travel Requirements

- Are you willing to relocate?
- In what region of the country or world would you be most comfortable?
- Would you like to be in a rural, suburban, or metropolitan area?
- How much travel are you willing to take on? What is your maximum percentage of travel (overnights per month)? Your frequency and duration of extended travel? Would you prefer working from your home office?

How else could you describe the exact job that you want? Add your own general criteria of your ideal job and add specific preferences.

When you have completed your list of job requirements, weight how important each area is for you. Go back over your ideal job listing, and do the same thing companies do when they put their job listings together. Of the important items on your list, mark those items that are not negotiable, very important, or simply nice-to-haves. Being very clear on your nonnegotiables will be especially helpful in eliminating job opportunities that will not work for you.

There is no limit to the value that will come from spending focused time on defining your ideal job. Once you have your ideal job clearly defined in your mind, you will not look at job postings or recommendations or search professional calls simply hoping that the right thing might come along. Eliminating job opportunities that you know will not work may be one of the greatest time- and resource-saving strategies that you can apply to your race for selection.

STEP THREE: DEFINE YOUR TWO- TO THREE-YEAR CAREER OBJECTIVES

The best way to start framing your two- to three-year career objectives is to answer three specific questions. Your response to these questions will set the tone for your career objectives as you identify the resources and opportunities necessary to prepare you for that plan. Keep in mind that these objectives will shape a specific action plan so it's good to have very few key bullet points:

1. Assuming that you have accepted your position in your ideal job listing, where do you see yourself growing in this position in two to three years?
2. What is fundamentally different in your job accountabilities in two to three years in terms of scope, complexity, and accountability? Carefully consider the ideal breadth of your job including span of control, functional oversight, and reporting structure.
3. What are the fundamentally different leadership demands of your job accountabilities in two to three years (greater involvement in people development, strategic planning, profit and loss accountability, etc.)?

Once you've answered these three questions, it is important to write a brief statement about your two- to three-year career goals that includes the key knowledge and experiences that you will need to be successful in that role. There are forms and examples of these exercises available on the Million-Dollar Race website (www. TheMillionDollarRace.com).

ENGAGING SIGNIFICANT OTHERS IN YOUR IDEAL JOB DESCRIPTION

Working through the preparation phase of the job search can be an isolating process. It is a common style for individuals to protect family and significant others from the day-to-day trials and tribulations of the job search process with the intent of sparing them the stress.

The challenge here is that the eventual outcome of the job-selection process will profoundly impact all of those who live with or depend on you in some way. It is not uncommon for an individual to successfully land a job offer and then find out that their family or partner is not supportive of the decision. Relocation tends to be the most common stumbling point.

A better strategy is to actively engage your significant others in active and open discussions about your job search from the beginning. As you build your ideal job listing and work criteria, it is highly useful to get the perspectives of those who will be impacted by the decision. Key areas for discussion include:

- What are the implications of a potential relocation and is that an eventuality that people can accept?
- What are the potential travel requirements for the new position and how will this impact your time at home?
- What are the hopes and potential fears that others are experiencing related to the job search?

The people you care about are far more adaptable to navigating changes in which they have an active input and opportunity to process their related feelings. Providing opportunities for regular and open discussions about your job search process is essential to finding a solution that will work for everyone impacted by the eventual outcome. Use your best judgment as a parent to bring children into the conversation on a level consistent with their age and maturity.

Taking the time to develop your ideal job description is an exercise that may take you as little as ninety minutes to complete. This simple document can be a powerful tool to keep your job search on a steady course and is well worth the investment. You will have a remarkable number of choices to weigh and having a clear standard by which to evaluate those options will be consistently useful. Once you have completed your ideal job description, print it out and post

Answer the Relocation Question Early and Clearly

There are two huge factors that will impact your ability to source job opportunities: time and your ability and willingness to relocate (or extend your commute). The longer you look for a job, the more possibilities you will uncover. The more you are willing to commute or relocate, the more positions are available in any given timeframe. This tradeoff is simply a matter of probability, and, depending on your current location and local job market, relocation may be a serious consideration for you.

Relocation is a significant challenge if you own a home or have family, social networks, kids in school, or a working partner. This is why it is so important to carefully think through the implications of relocation very early in your job search. It is easy to avoid this difficult question, hoping that it will not be an issue. The longer a search continues the more pressure candidates experience to consider relocation.

Weigh the options, including financial, social, emotional, and transition challenges. The more you openly and deliberately think this through, the more actively you can shape this critical factor in your job search.

it in your office area or place it in a top drawer where you can refer to it often. You will find that the language translates naturally into your networking conversations and online profiles. Your consistent messaging will take you to your desired destination.

QUESTIONS FOR REFLECTION

There is no better time than the beginning of the race to get grounded in what winning looks like. It only takes an hour or two hours to create an ideal job description. Doing so can save you many, many hours of work and potential frustration. Invest that time now.

- Are you a visually creative person? If so, it may make more sense for you to create a picture board using graphic images rather than the written plan. If this idea naturally appeals to you, consider creating a collage of images that represent your ideal career path. This might give you the creative impetus to follow-up on a more detailed, written plan.

- What are the three most important values you hold for an optimal career path? What values are most likely to drive your success and your contentment? Are you willing to make the potentially tough decisions necessary to see that these values are realized?
- How will you build accountability and follow-through once you create your ideal description? Will you tell friends and colleagues about your ideal position, and will you make a specific commitment to reviewing your ideal job description on a monthly basis?
- What else could you do besides creating an ideal job description that would provide you direction, inspiration, and accountability to make the decisions necessary to obtain your ideal career path?

CHAPTER FOUR
Define Your Ideal Organization

The next step is to make an active choice about the kind of organization you want to work for. This is a crucially important part of the preparation process. At no other time in the selection process will you be as completely in control of determining the ideal organization that will provide an optimal fit for your skills and preferred culture.

Online dating sites ask you to fill out a questionnaire about your personality and interests as a way to ensure the best match for a partner. In this step of preparation you will consider the very nature of your ideal hiring organization.

DEFINING YOURSELF AS THE BUYER

As you develop your mindset in approaching your job search, it is essential that you approach any target organization from the perspective of the buyer. *You* are the one who makes the first decision in the selection process. If a particular job opportunity does not meet your career goals, location, or financial requirements, or other features identified as "nonnegotiables," you should quickly eliminate that opportunity from your pool.

Make this a regular practice in your job search and you will reinforce a critical aspect of mindset. Until you complete an application or submit a résumé, you *are* the buyer. When you start eliminating job opportunities based only on what you think is most important to you, you are in control of the job search process.

Think about the process of buying a car. If you go car shopping with little idea about what you want in a car or how much you want to spend, you are more vulnerable to getting caught up in an emotional decision orchestrated by a savvy salesperson and sales manager. You are more likely to buy a car that strikes you as beautiful, fast, or some other attribute based on your feelings in the moment. The likely result is buyer's remorse. Recruiters are highly skilled salespeople. Chances are that experienced recruiters can create a compelling reason for you to consider an organization, even if you know that the culture or job accountabilities are not a strong fit for you.

CONDUCTING RESEARCH AS A BUYER

As in any research project, it is essential that you determine the scope, depth, and resources necessary to build a successful research process. As a starting point, consider the following five areas of inquiry as an organizing framework for your research as the buyer of your next job opportunity.

FILTER ONE: DOMINANT FUNCTIONS

A powerful step toward helping you understand the "personality" of an organization is to understand which organizational function has been dominant in the recent direction of the organization and how that function relates to your career interests.

In some cases, the gap between your career path and the dominant culture of the organization can be a wonderful thing. Many organizations understand what they are missing and actively seek individuals who will help them grow in new directions. In other cases, people in nondominant functions are the "odd people out" and struggle for acceptance and inclusion.

Consider the following six functional areas as potential dominant functions and how they potentially shape leadership, growth, and decision making and how your interest and background may fit or be a potential stretch.

Finance-Led Organizations

Finance can be a dominant culture in any organization, especially when the holding structure is private ownership or equity partner ownership. In these cases the current valuation of the organization is of paramount importance. This means that most organizational decisions, including the recapitalization, expansion, acquisition, etc., will be made based on their immediate impact on the income statement and balance sheet. Every decision will filter through financial analysis.

Implications for You

If you're not in finance you would be well served to get a good grounding in financial analysis and accounting as you will be expected to understand and make decisions based on financial implications. In the interview process, you will likely be assessed directly or indirectly on your financial literacy. If you know this is an area of opportunity for you, it may be a good investment to take a course on finance for non-financial managers or brush up on your college or MBA textbooks.

Sales-Led Organizations

In the sales organization, the entire growth engine is based primarily on acquiring new business. In this case, the sales organization leads the organization and most of the functions, including product or service development; operations are completely focused on what the organization sells. Sales-based organizations tend to be fun, upbeat, and interactive places to work. They can also be highly competitive and driven. Be prepared to unabashedly sell yourself in the interview process. People who run a sales-based organization are typically looking for "hunter/closers" who speak up directly, make eye contact, and ask for the sale.

Implications for You

As a good friend of mine says, "In business, we are all teachers and we are all salespeople." If you have any prejudices or negative attributes associated with selling or salespeople, it would be good to reexamine these assumptions prior to joining the sales-based organization. Sales-based organizations tend to move quickly, focus on relationships, and set competitive standards. If this is not a fit for you and your relational style, it would be good to think of some adaptive strategies or think about a different kind of organization.

Marketing-Led Organizations

In these organizations marketing typically takes the lead in determining product and service mix based on understanding customer demands. This kind of organization is typically organized around a very strong product management framework that includes accountability for product and market segmentation, pricing, and product strategy. Being close to product development and the workflow through the organization to take this product to market is typically the most engaging and appreciated role within this kind of organization.

Implications for You

If you are a salesperson looking at a marketing-based organization, you will want to fully understand the relationship between sales and marketing as part of your interview process. In many cases a strong marketing function works well with a strong sales force, with marketing people managing product or service lines working harmoniously with salespeople to manage customer accounts. In some cases, these working relationships have not been defined consistently and you may be entering into an age-old dispute that tends to shape sales and marketing relationships.

Engineering-Led Organizations

Engineering-based organizations typically evolved from the brilliant inventor/entrepreneur who started the organization or a new technology in which the organization invested. These are organizations that have consistently differentiated themselves in the market by developing new products and processes that set them apart. Whether the product of consideration is a hay bailer or rocket telemetry equipment, an engineering-based organization tends to attract people who have a natural interest and energy for new projects and for all things technical.

Implications for You

Engineering-based organizations can be highly chaotic especially at the start-up stages of the business process. If the organization has not reached profitability, cash flows and investments are treated with great care. If there is a need to cut expenses in these organizations, it makes sense to make the initial cuts outside the area considered most important for producing future revenues. This means that sales and engineering are going to get top billing in the organization, and other functions such as HR or marketing may not get the same status or prioritization.

Operations-Led Organizations

These organizations focus on manufacturing, supply chain, and/or service delivery efficiencies as the basis of competitive advantage.

Operations-led organizations decisions are made primarily on maintaining or growing market share based on cost, quality, speed of delivery, and overall production efficiency. Many of these organizations focus their culture around key aspects of high-efficiency (or "Lean") manufacturing, safety, and cost control.

Implications for You

Expect that many of the decisions of the organization will be filtered through operational efficiencies and supply-chain optimization. You would be well served to be familiar with the basics of lean manufacturing principles and eminently familiar with words like "Gemba," "Kaizen," "5S," and "Kanban." You may also find that an operations-based organization has taken a pencil to corporate salaries and is looking for the greatest value in the job market.

Human Resources–Led Organizations

Human resources (HR) as a dominant culture is more prevalent in direct-to-consumer service industries, entertainment, and big-box retail, which tends to invest much of their operating expenses into people selection, training, and payroll. These organizations by their very nature are highly focused on the dynamics of people to achieve desired outcomes.

HR-dominated organizations tend to be focused on stability and fairness to employees as the basis of maintaining and retaining a strong and reliable workforce. In some cases HR organizations tend to be more relaxed and seem less competitive than their counterparts.

Implications for You

HR-led organizations can be fun places to work, provided that you are not driven to change things quickly within your target role. HR-oriented organizations tend to have a great deal of stability established through careful documentation, process, and procedure. This should be a good fit if you have patience and you need a stable, long-term work situation. On the other hand, if you are a mover and shaker and are driven to take an organization in new directions quickly, you may find yourself at odds with the culture of a typical HR-led organization.

Understanding the dominant functions within an organization will help you understand a great deal about its culture and modus operandi in getting things done. Here are four questions to ask to help you quickly determine which functions may shape and drive organizational dynamics:

1. Through which function did the CEO or owner of the organization rise?
2. What function is seen as leading to the greatest differentiation of the organization in a competitive marketplace?
3. Which function's offices are located near the executive suite and how big and how many windows do people in that function typically have?
4. Which functions have a seat at the executive table for the highest-level executive team and lead major corporate initiatives?

In most cases you will find the dominant function represented as the answer to most if not all these questions.

FILTER TWO: OWNERSHIP

Ownership structure of the organization will greatly determine internal dynamics and culture. As most organizations will bend to the needs and purpose of the owners, it is vital that you understand who the owners are and what their primary expectations for organizational performance might be. Listed next are some of the most common holding structures. For each holding structure there is a definition and implications for you as a potential job candidate.

Private and/or Family Owned

Privately owned organizations are held by an individual, groups of individuals, or families, typically as some type of private corporation.

Implications for You

From a job seeker's perspective, private or family-owned organizations, particularly those in the first or second generation of owners, tend to be a clear expression of the individual entrepreneur or group of entrepreneurs that started the organization. Individual entrepreneurs tend to run organizations that are idiosyncratic in the way they have built and been successful with the organization. In some cases those individuals exhibit a strong command-and-control management style and tend to be deeply ingrained as influential in the day-to-day operations of the business.

Within family-owned organizations, there can be complex—and in some cases challenging—dynamics as second- or third-generation children or extended families become involved in the ownership or management of the organization. As the original founders grow older there can be an unsettling movement to either a more stable, professional management structure or a shift in leadership structure to family members who are vying for control and ownership.

Organizations can take a very long time to move from a family structure and can easily grow to multibillion-dollar industries—often retaining the signature dynamics of a mom-and-pop shop.

Recommended Research Action

As privately owned organizations are not required to publish financials or annual reports, it is more difficult to do objective research. In this case you will need to rely on news articles, employee reviews, and general company reviews available in databases. During the application and selection process it is very useful to keep your ears and eyes open for signs of disruption, transition, and change, all of which can be for the eventual good of the organization and can also be challenging to maneuver, especially as an outside leader coming into a family-run organization.

Private Equity Owned

The majority of the shares of a private equity owned organization are held by an individual or group of investors.

Implications for You

It is critically important to understand that private equity investors make their investment for one reason: they expect to sell at a profit sometime in the future. The entire debt structure of the company and financial strategy of the organization are built on this premise.

What this inevitably means for you is that there will be a sale and/or additional acquisitions in the organization, potentially in a two- to seven-year time frame from the original acquisition. This may be less of a concern for line management positions that are embedded in specific business units. For corporate or other staff positions, the sale of the organization typically means a merger or acquisition in which staff positions are at far greater risk for reduction in force.

Recommended Research Actions

Determine who the equity partner(s) are. Do some research on their additional holdings and find out the typical length of time they hold companies before selling. Is their strategy to grow their holding through acquisitions or simply focus on organic growth as a potential source of value? Remember that privately held organizations do not publish financial records as do publicly held organizations. You may have to dig a little harder on your research here.

Publicly Held Corporation

Publicly held companies have some part of their shares available through stock exchange and are traded on an active basis. As such, the primary objective of a publicly held company is to provide value to the shareholders. This typically means increasing the value of various issues of stock or pay out of dividends based on superior financial performance.

Implications for You

One of the primary purposes of a publicly held organization is to build shareholder value for the individuals, investors, and fund managers who own shares in the organization. Publicly held companies tend to make very different business decisions from private or private equity owned organizations in that they tend to have a longer timeframe for the investment.

At the same time, there is consistent consideration of financial decisions that will impact share value, so it cannot be assumed that all decisions will be long term. While most publicly held organizations are susceptible to acquisitions and mergers, that outcome may be less central to the original ownership agenda. Publicly traded companies can be a more stable place to work than private equity firms as there is not an embedded need to make short-term financial decisions to make the organization more attractive to the market.

Recommended Research Action

From a research perspective, one of the great advantages of considering a publicly traded company is that there is a vast array of documentation, including annual reports, 10-Ks, analysts' reports, and extensive financial media coverage that provides a wealth of information on these organization. A list of key resources available to the public is listed at the conclusion of this chapter.

Employee Stock Ownership Plan

The employee stock ownership plan (ESOP) is a type of trust in which the employee benefits from investments from the employer. The firm sets up a trust and makes tax-deductible donations, and full-time employees with a minimum amount of service can be included in the plan. Employees can also contribute a percentage of their salaries to the plan. The ESOP offers additional tax incentives to both the employer and employee.

Implications for You

ESOPs and other varieties of employee-owned companies offer unique investment opportunities and tax advantages. Joining a successful organization with an ESOP could pave the road to a healthy retirement, or at least a sizable contribution. The main drawback of an ESOP program is that it can potentially tie up a large portion of the employees' investments in a single organization. This means if something negative should happen to the organization on a wide scale, employees would likely lose a large percentage of their investments. At a time when huge and successful organizations commonly wither due to scandal, poor financial planning, or rapid changes in economic conditions, diversification of investments, including employee benefit plans, should be a rule of thumb regardless of a particular organization's offerings.

Recommended Research Actions

There are currently about 11,500 ESOPs, including 11 million employees in the United States, almost all in private, closely held companies. This means that statements of financial performance are generally not publicly accessible. If considering an organization that offers an ESOP, it would be wise to ask for as much information as possible about the financial performance of the organization at later stages of the interview process. As tempting as it may be to put all your long-term investments toward an organization for which you work, diversification in retirement planning will always be the wisest choice.

Nonprofit or Not-for-profit Organizations

There is often confusion between the terms "nonprofit" and "not-for-profit." There are indeed both legal and accounting differences between the two, but a true distinction quickly becomes technical. In general, a not-for-profit organization is never designed to make profit. In contrast, a nonprofit organization may have a charitable cause at the core of its mission, but it is able to create and retain profits.

Implications for You

The first thing to consider if you are looking into nonprofits for the first time is the salary range. The spread is typically 20 percent to 50 percent lower for similar levels and scope of accountability compared with corporations.

Many people are attracted to the idea of a nonprofit organization with the premise that these organizations are far more laid-back, relaxed, and less competitive than their for-profit counterparts. The idea of getting out of the rat race and into an organization mission and purpose that is aligned with their values is appealing.

The reality is that profit orientation has little to do with the dynamics within an organization. Federal dollars, grant money, and jobs in general are tight. The result is paid positions in nonprofit or not-for-profit are as competitive as for-profit organizations. The culture of nonprofits can be equally competitive.

Recommended Research Actions

The best place to start with research on a not-for-profit, nonprofit, or a heavily volunteer-based organization is to understand its place in a regional, national, or international organizational structure. Large not-for-profit organizations can be as sophisticated and bureaucratic as for-profit corporations in terms of layers of management, reporting relationships, and divisional structures. Develop a clear understanding of how embedded or autonomous the specific area you are targeting for career opportunity is within the "mothership."

Take a close look at the financial stability of a particular organization. Beginning with the economic slowdown, charity-based organizations that rely predominantly on fundraising have been hit heavily. In order to maintain service levels, they have cut staff or asked their staff to take salary reductions on the basis of maintaining their contribution rates. It would be good to analyze whether the financial situation is workable given your lifestyle expectations.

FILTER THREE: ORGANIZATIONAL MATURITY

One of the best ways to understand where an organization is going is to understand where it has been. Organizational dynamics and culture often follow the same pattern over time. Organizations move through predictable stages of birth, childhood, adolescence, adulthood, and eventual old age. In many cases, organizations exhibit all the characteristics we would expect at a given stage of maturity. For example, start-up organizations that are just beginning to establish their workflows and customer relationships can often resemble a two-year-old jumping off into any direction that seems interesting at the time with boundless energy and seemingly little discipline or direction.

As an organization progresses to maturity, systems and processes change. The organization tends to slowly (and sometimes painfully) implement processes and procedures to standardize work and focus strategy and work outputs accordingly. In doing your buy-side analysis, it is critically important to understand what phase of development your organization is in at the time it is under your consideration. Consider the stages of an organization as defined in Table 4.1.

Review the definitions in this table. Which stage is most descriptive of the organization or division that you are targeting for selection? Is this organization a cultural fit for you?

A good thing to keep in mind is that the larger the organization, the more slowly it progresses from one stage to the next. For example, a start-up with a strong operations function can move quickly from childhood to adolescence (within a year to three years), whereas transformation from early to late adulthood may take over a decade.

FILTER FOUR: ORGANIZATIONAL REPORTING STRUCTURE

The organizational reporting structure refers to how the organization is organized in terms of major operating units and geographic locations. Smaller organizations (typically with fewer than five hundred employees) may have a very simple structure with an executive group, including a president or CEO overseeing a set of functional areas within a single business unit. As an organization becomes larger and more complex, there can be many levels that are based on geographic regions or product or service lines. Some very large, multinational organizations have both geographic and line of business latticework in their reporting structure.

Understand the general reporting structure surrounding the job environment in a particular business unit or corporate role you are considering. In broad terms, you might consider if the general reporting structure is either hierarchical or flat and if the immediate

Table 4.1: Stages of Organizational Development

Stage of Development	Typical Cultural Implications
1. Birth	Brand-new start-up typically led by high-energy entrepreneurial individual or small team; high-energy, chaotic, long hours, creativity, sense of community, high financial risk/high reward.
2. Childhood	Emergent systems and processes, people focus, balancing growth versus cash flow, fast growth. Sales and operations or service delivery are dominant functions. Potential pace of growth outpacing structures and bandwidth of people resulting in chaos. Cash flow crises are common.
3. Adolescence	Searching for core meaning and strategy, exploration of alternative revenue streams, sometimes resulting in poor or painful decisions, initial or build out of internal systems and processes, initial acquisitions; steep growth in revenues and people resources; desire to expand requires additional infusion of capital.
4. Early Adulthood	High-performance, dialing in on product/service mix, further acquisition or integration of other entities, initial professionalization of management skills, differentiation of functional units, standardization of systems and processes. Initial international expansion.
5. Late Adulthood or Maturity	Emergence of corporate structure and strategic business units, specializations within functions, centralized sourcing and shared services model for human resources, finance, IT, etc.; integration of centralized information systems or outsourcing of functions. Robust international expansion; potential Initial public offering.
6. Old Age	Transition in leadership, increasing levels of management, bureaucracy, lack of renewal, political infighting, loss of market share to more nimble competitors, active or passive choices made between renewal and decline.

reporting structure related to the job you're considering is either direct or matrixed.

One of the most significant implications for hierarchal vs. flat and matrixed reporting structures has to do with the degree of autonomy and speed of making decisions.

In hierarchical structure, there is a need to sell and build approval for most ideas, and the resulting decreased speed in decision making and implementation. Individuals who have functioned autonomously invariably feel constrained, frustrated, and anxious if they have not carefully recalibrated their leadership styles to accommodate the changing pace.

Individuals operating successfully in leadership roles in these kinds of organizations may have multiple layers of reporting structure. For example, if you are in a staff position in finance, you may have a direct reporting relationship with the executive vice president for finance as well as an indirect reporting relationship to a strategic business unit president, and business unit accounting staff may have a dotted line reporting relationship to you.

Project-based organizations such as engineering or consulting firms can also have dynamic reporting structures in that individuals maintain a fairly flat reporting structure within the context of a time-limited project. This dynamic could translate into having a new boss every few months and a new set of coworkers depending on the size, scope, and technical demands of a particular project. If your preference is for highly stable, long-term working relationships with a set number of colleagues, this environment may not be a good fit.

FILTER FIVE: THE FUTURE OF THE ORGANIZATION

If you plan to stay with this organization for more than a year or two, it would be especially helpful to understand where the organization is headed in the future. Here are some typical questions to consider:

- What are the organization's growth prospects for the next five years?
- What new products or service offerings and what corresponding new markets might be developed?
- What are the emerging market conditions for the future of this organization?
- What is the current geographical footprint of the company and what geographical markets will be pursued?
- How does the macro economic forecast weigh in on the profitability of this organization? What would happen in a major upturn or downturn in the economy?
- What is the probability that jobs will be offshored or transferred due to international expansion?
- How close to retirement are the senior leadership teams, and who will likely be their successors? How stable has the senior leadership team been over the last five years?
- What is the likelihood that this organization will acquire, merge, or be acquired by other organizations?
- What would be the implication of any of these events for your target position?

These questions can be answered through careful research. In these days of rapid technological changes, fast-moving economies, and industry consolidation, there is far less stability in organizational structures. You may be attracted to change, and you may be pleased with a two- to three-year stint. If not, you may want to make an active choice to seek larger, more conservative and stable organizations.

RESEARCHING ORGANIZATIONAL CULTURE

Most job boards and a few specific websites (e.g., GlassDoor.com and LinkedIn.com) offer free reviews of current or former employees' written recommendations of organizations. These reviews can provide a useful insight into the day-to-day experience that employees have had during their time with the organization. While these reviews can provide meaningful information, you should use this information only as one point in your research. Keep in mind these limitations of online job reviews:

- People who write job reviews may be motivated by a negative experience or by separation from the company and may have an axe to grind.
- People who write job reviews may have perceptions shaped by a negative experience with a direct supervisor, which may have no bearing on your current position.

Pay most attention when there are a large number of consistent reviews that summarize the same issue. You should minimize the weight you put on any single review, especially if it sounds like a tirade or an emotional response to a specific negative event.

Another useful technique is to use your LinkedIn or other network connections to find people who work in the organization. Drop them a note saying that you are interested in their organization and you would like to get their candid opinion of what it's like to work there. Ask them specifically about their organization's values. Most people are intrigued by the question and will be pleased to share fifteen minutes with you.

Free Sources of Company Information on the Web

Source	Description
Company website	Company websites include company description, locations, values, mission, culture, history, products/services, contact information, and much more. If the company is public, see the website's "Investor Relations" section, which will include financial reports, annual reports, press releases, and presentations to their investors.
Glassdoor.com	Past or current employees share experiences, reviews, salaries, and what you can expect in an interview.
Google.com	Google search is a great way to find high-traffic areas for blogs and other sources such as press releases, news articles, and financial reports.
Manta.com	Manta.com is an established company research site with variable quality of information. The site is supported primarily through advertisements, so you will need to hunt for information. The site includes key contacts in the organization.
SlideShare.com	Users upload presentations/documents on companies and specific topics. There is a good chance you will come across some information on the company you are researching on this site.
LinkedIn.com	You can find brief descriptions of companies on LinkedIn. In addition there are discussion forums, which include candid comments about the organization, salaries, and culture.

Understanding the culture of an organization is essential if you are going to find a solid fit. The nature of an organization based on history, structure, values, and business model is likely to be stable. While people can adapt to a predominant culture over time, a significant difference between your needs and the personality of the organization will most likely lead to frustrations and stress in day-to-day work experiences. This will become increasingly apparent after the initial "honeymoon" phase of the relationship.

Taking the time to consider cultural implications is an essential part of your discipline of preparation. The initial temptation to compromise based on the need to fill a role quickly by the organization and the need to get a high-paying job by the candidate can result in unhealthy compromises on both sides. The result can be a turbulent relationship that results in an eventual parting of ways. In contrast, people who are well suited to their organizational environments find consistent sources of energy and reinforcement in their match and reinforcement with organizational culture.

QUESTIONS FOR REFLECTION

Organizational culture is one of the key components of fit. Having a solid idea of what day-to-day life is going to be like in your target organization is well worth the consideration:

- Imagine you are arriving at work on a perfect day in the future. What does the organization look like? Create a clear mental image of your ideal organization and work back through the filters to be clear about your preferences.
- What have you learned from your past that you clearly want to avoid in a future organizational setting? What type of organization is most likely going to present that dynamic?
- How much latitude and free rein do you need in your

management style? Will organizational constraints—including approvals, committees, and top-down reviews—drive you crazy? If so, you may consider removing mature, highly structured organizations from your hit list.

- What is your career history relative to functional experience? If you have come up through a single function or a few related functions, will that history be honored and appreciated at the executive table? As you reflect on your organizational filter list, what organization features are nonnegotiable and what are key areas on which you can bend given the right opportunities in other areas?

CHAPTER FIVE

Assessing Yourself: The Johari Window

UNDERSTANDING YOURSELF

The fourth area of preparation is approaching the selection race with a balanced and objective understanding of yourself, your capabilities, and strengths as well as your limitations, untested areas, and needs for development. Another remarkably useful area of self-understanding is based on your personality style or "preferences," which refer to your natural patterns of working with people and information and drawing conclusions.

THE JOHARI WINDOW: A POWERFUL TOOL OF SELF-UNDERSTANDING

In the vast sea of consulting tools and frameworks, there are a few choice tools that never grow old and never outlive their usefulness. The Johari Window is such a tool. (See Table 5.1.) Used effectively, the Window can help an individual build a powerful perspective on how you see yourself and how others see you. The Johari Window was created by Joseph Luft and Harry Ingham in 1955. Since that time it has been used extensively in corporate settings and self-help groups to help individuals develop a more balanced perspective.

Perception is a very complex phenomenon. Perception can very often be created and maintained by conclusions that are formed on partial or low-quality information. Perceptions about you are important in preparing for the selection race in that these perspectives will shape the way that you see yourself as well as the self that you project to talent agents, recruiters, and hiring managers. Taking charge of shaping and directing these perceptions will enable you to lead your own selection campaign.

Table 5.1: The Johari Window

	Known to self	Not known to self
Known to others	Frame One, The Arena: Perceptions that are clearly shared by you and others.	Frame Two, Blind Spots: Perceptions that others have of you that you do not know.
Not known to others	Frame Four, The Façade: perceptions of you that you hide from others	Frame Three, The Unknown: Perceptions that have not been formed based on lack of experience or understanding by yourself and others.

FRAME ONE, THE ARENA

The first frame of the Johari Window refers to perceptions that are clear and consistent between yourself and others. These are aspects of your behavior and personality that are readily observable and support a consistent interpretation and conclusion about who you are. You might be known by yourself and others as an affable, open, and generous individual. You may also be known by yourself and others to be shrewd, distant, and calculating. Work in Frame One includes defining your personal brand or establishing the set of perspectives you wish to project to others.

FRAME TWO, BLIND SPOTS

The second frame of the Johari Window includes perceptions that others have formed about you of which you have limited knowledge or insight. If you have blind spots that are clear to others, it is best to bring these areas to light before you get to the selection process.

People can work in highly structured work settings for decades with blind spots. Cultural norms and expectations direct us away from providing clear, accurate, and timely feedback to others. As an individual moves up to progressively higher levels of the organization and gains power and authority, coworkers are likely to avoid providing feedback for fear of retribution or simply from discomfort with challenging conversations.

FRAME THREE, THE UNKNOWN

The Unknown includes perceptions of you that are not known because they have not been formed. In the context of the selection process these are skills and capabilities that you have not demon-strated because you have not been in the situation that required them. A good example of this is how you might perform in a posi-tion that is at the level above where you are right now. In terms of the selection process, it is important that most selection considerations include not only the immediate job that you will fill, but also the higher-level positions that you could fill in the next two to five years.

FRAME FOUR, THE FAÇADE

The Façade includes perceptions that you have of yourself that are not shared with others because you make an active choice to shape or hide the behaviors that would generate these perceptions. The Façade has both a light and a dark side. On the light side, we all have knowledge about ourselves, our proclivities, and past behaviors that we know to be negative or disruptive. We learn from an early stage of maturity to temper, manage, or hide these aspects of ourselves. We may have a natural tendency to be irritable, judgmental, selfish, or vindictive. A key aspect of adult behavior is the ability to understand unconstructive drives and resulting behaviors and avoid the negative impact of expressing these.

USING THE JOHARI WINDOW IN SELECTION PREPARATION

The Johari Window can be a powerful tool as you prepare for the selection process. Each frame of the window suggests specific oppor-tunities to increase your total self-awareness or, at the very least, define what you do not know and what you can learn more about.

Below are descriptions of each frame of the Johari Window and some specific strategies and tools that you can employ to address each area in your preparation for selection. On a blank piece of paper, draw out the four quadrants and label each section. As you read through this chapter, take notes in each quadrant based on your initial thoughts and insights.

FRAME ONE, THE ARENA: ESTABLISHING YOUR PERSONAL BRAND

Branding is the filter by which people shape their expectations for future benefit based on established credibility. We are all familiar with the power and value of commercial brands. Powerful brands create powerful expectations among consumers who are willing to spend significantly more money for consistency, quality, durability, and status.

If you are selling yourself for potentially $1 million or more on the open job market, it would serve you well to be extremely clear and articulate about your personal brand. Effective branding includes these three attributes:

1. Expresses clear value in terms of what is important to the customer.
2. Clearly distinguishes you from your competition.
3. Is presented in a concise and elegant way.

So how do you go about establishing and articulating your personal brand? One of the fastest and easiest ways to begin is to distill the message of your unique value to the shortest and cleanest expression possible. Every sales, marketing, political strategy, or advertising professional knows the power of the tagline or the elevator speech in establishing consistent introduction to the market. If the message is not clear and concise and an entrée into a compelling story, there is no reason why anyone would take the time or be inclined to take action relative to the message.

That moment is no time to begin fumbling for words or descriptions that have not been carefully constructed and practiced. An elevator speech is by no means a canned or rote memorized two sentences that are to be blurted out at any opportunity. An elevator speech is driven by your ability to quickly deliver the core message of your unique brand, which has been shaped to meet the needs of any opportunity. This results in a fresh, spontaneous, and genuine delivery, because you've invested hours in crafting the message.

What are the key defining attributes of your brand to be included in your elevator speech? Write these down in the "Arena" section of your Johari Window. Consider how this branding shows up in your day-to-day interactions, your dress, your speech, and your mannerisms. There are specific exercises in chapter six of this book to help you establish your brand message.

FRAME TWO, BLIND SPOTS: GETTING CONSTRUCTIVE FEEDBACK

Throughout my career, I've had the opportunity to provide one-on-one feedback sessions based on 360 feedback tools (assessments that are completed by people who work for an individual, their boss, their peers, and themselves) to hundreds of managers and executives. Often the 360 feedback is the first time individuals hear information about their unproductive or offensive behaviors. In some cases, this gap between self-perception and the perception of others has persisted for decades. Some individuals are devastated by the feedback.

The challenge of blind spots is that if you have them, by definition you don't know you have them. The only way to discover blind spots is to receive clear, unbiased, and direct feedback on your behaviors. There are at least two ways of effectively getting this kind of feedback, one formal and one informal. The 360 report includes ratings of key behaviors or competencies that have been shown by

Beware of Career Derailers

There actually is a well-researched list of career derailers that often appear as blind spots that have been shown to end or limit a career. This hit list, based on research from the Center for Creative Leadership, includes these major areas:

1. **Handling the demands of the management job:** This includes all the necessary attributes to get one's current accountabilities accomplished completely and quickly, including resourcefulness, commitment, learning quickly, and making timely decisions. In many cases, these derailers emerge from lack of formal training in management skills, including time management, process control, financial planning, and resource allocation.

2. **Dealing with subordinates:** This derailer includes leading subordinates effectively through delegation and fairness, creating a developmental climate where subordinates can grow, confronting performance issues quickly, developing a positive team atmosphere, and hiring the right people for the team.

3. **Respect for self and others:** This includes building and maintaining positive relationships, having compassion and sensitivity for others, demonstrating mature composure, finding appropriate work balance, being self-aware of strengths and opportunities for development, displaying warmth and sense of humor, and acting with flexibility to meet the demands of the situation.

("Preventing Derailment: What to Do Before It's too Late" by Michael M. Lombardo and Robert W. Eichinger, Greensboro, North Carolina: Center for Creative Leadership, 1989.)

No doubt as you review this list you can think of previous or current bosses or other individuals within your organization who have fallen down due to a lack of commitment or understanding of these critical performance areas. If you are not completely clear on what these opportunities might be or how these behaviors are perceived by others, you may have a significant blind spot. As you prepare for the selection race, there is no better time to isolate these factors and begin a plan to remedy these attributes with a sound development plan.

research to define performance at the management level and typi-cally open-ended responses that give the reader an opportunity to express candid feedback on your leadership style.

Another unsettling aspect of blind spots is that they frequently lead to career derailment or job termination. Because direct, con-structive, and powerful feedback is an extremely rare commodity in today's organizations, individuals get blocked in their careers because of personal quirks or temperaments that inevitably inhibit their abil-ity to gain the trust, influence, or credibility to get things accom-plished in the organization. Rather than addressing these limitations head-on, people with fatal blind spots are often sidelined, kicked up, kicked out, or ignored.

If you are not presently in a work situation, you can still conduct a 360 using an online tool. You would simply need to find a number of people with whom you worked in the past and invite them to complete a brief assessment online. Several of these tools are avail-able online. The 3D Group is a highly valuable vendor of this service: www.3dgroup.net. A 360 feedback report can be one of the most powerful tools you can use in preparing for the selection process since the report typically uncovers areas of opportunity for you to develop for which you may have had no or little previous awareness.

Another avenue to receive feedback is a direct and open conver-sation with people you have interacted with in a work situation. This is a less rigorous and standardized approach, but in a few conversa-tions you can still identify some very specific areas of strengths and opportunities on which you can build. Doing an informal verbal 360 can produce meaningful results.

FRAME THREE, THE UNKNOWN: UNDERSTANDING YOUR FUTURE POTENTIAL

Frame Three of the Johari Window, the "Unknown," focuses on what is not known about the individual by themselves or by others. In the

Conducting a Self-Initiated, Verbal 360 Discussion

By definition, a blind spot is an area in which you have not received consistent or accurate feedback. Getting more information about your blind spots can be a challenging process.

While an external perspective will add a great deal of value, a self-initiated verbal 360 requires some thought, sensitivity, and planning to perform successfully. Following is a suggested format for conducting this activity:

1. Select three to five people with whom you've worked in the past and with whom you have a strong sense of rapport and trust. It is most helpful if these people have had the opportunity to directly observe your day-to-day work behaviors and represent different kinds of relationships with you, including direct reports, peers, bosses, and internal or external customers.

2. Explain to each of these individuals that you would like to set up a conversation of up to thirty minutes to help you understand how you can become a better leader. If it makes sense and is within the realm of prudent confidentiality, explain that you're doing this in preparation for job selection.

3. Meet with each individual in a quiet, private, and uninterrupted setting. Explain that you would like to get some candid and thoughtful feedback on your work behaviors and that you are collecting this information to improve your performance, and if appropriate, prepare for your job search.

4. Begin the interview process by asking these broad and nondirective questions:

   - "What do you see as my strengths as a leader?"
   - "What should I stop doing to be a more effective leader?"
   - "What do you believe I can start doing to be a more effective leader in the future?"

These three questions should prime the pump for an open and candid conversation. If you trust the individual providing the feedback and they have trust and appreciation for you, you will most likely get high-quality feedback as well as enhance your relationship.

Allow the conversation to move freely, and be prepared to offer some follow-up prompts, such as, "What could I have done differently in that situation?" or "What have you seen others do in a similar situation that you think is highly effective?" Most importantly, never, ever refute the information you receive by offering explanations, excuses, or being in any way defensive. Your only response in a verbal 360 should be limited to "Thank you for that feedback" or simply ask for additional information to clarify a point made.

Compile your responses in notes and review the feedback that you receive from several people. Identify themes, especially those themes that may be uncomfortable or unsettling. The things that hit you as most surprising or difficult to accept are most likely your blind spots. Your resistance has probably created the blind spot in the first place.

Information collected from a self-initiated verbal 360 can produce highly effective information related to your blind spots. This information can be effectively harnessed in your selection preparation through developmental planning.

context of the job search and selection race, the key aspect of the unknown is your future potential to take on jobs and accountabilities in the organization for which you have no specific track record.

There are specific traits and competencies that have been identified as being predictive of future potential. The validity of assessments has saved organizations millions of dollars by more accurately predicting and selecting individuals who will be successful at the next level.

"Potential" is defined as the inherent ability to take on new tasks and seize opportunities without prior experience or extensive preparation. The learning agility construct has been shown to be predictive of future potential. Learning agility is the general ability to respond quickly and effectively to new and challenging situations. (*FYI for*

Learning Agility, Robert Eichinger, Michael Lombardo, and Cara C. Capretta, Korn/Ferry, 2010). This trait is reflected in an individual who can make the transition into a new level of management successfully through fast learning, personal insight, intelligence, and perseverance.

In general, you can get a sense of your own level of learning agility by reflecting back on every new level of job and accountability you have taken on in the past and thinking through these key questions:

- Were you able to take on an increase in workload and scope of accountability quickly and efficiently?
- Were you able to learn key leadership skills and capabilities that were essential to the new position or responsibility?
- Have you been able to effectively lead individuals who may have had more experience, technical knowledge, or seniority than you in a specific work area?
- Have you successfully managed a significant, negative event in your career history (e.g., significant downsizing, product failure, acquisition, personal or family trauma) and come out of that situation stronger and more adaptable than ever?

Answering yes to all of these is a good indication that you have high potential to move beyond your current level. Individuals with high potential are able to explain how they can cope quickly and what specific strategies they employ to respond to these challenges successfully. These traits are the underpinnings of potential. In your Johari Window, jot down those attributes that capture your capabilities related to learning agility in the "Unknown" quadrant.

FRAME FOUR, THE FAÇADE: WHAT DO YOU FILTER?

In the context of architecture, a façade is defined as the front of the building, especially an imposing or decorative one. All candidates vying for a million-dollar job will be carefully constructing a façade in the form of recommendations, cover letters, résumé, interviews, and other interactions with the potential hiring organizations to present themselves in the best light possible. As a job candidate you will need to make consistent decisions about how you construct and present your façade.

In many of the leadership seminars that I have led throughout my career, one of my favorite exercises is to ask the class, "What is the difference between leadership and manipulation?" At first it seems the difference would be obvious. Leadership is good and manipulation is bad. Leadership is a positive trait and manipulation is reprehensible. But how are actions and outcomes of these behaviors significantly different?

Most definitions of leadership include some ability to communicate a future state or objective and get individuals motivated to take action to achieve that objective. Certainly the same could be said for manipulation. Manipulation is also aimed at getting people to do what you want them to do. Some of the key differentiators that are often suggested include

- Leadership is open and honest, while manipulation is covert and subversive.
- Leadership is based on the truth, while manipulation may be based on lies.
- Leadership is focused on the needs of the whole organization, while manipulation is focused only on the needs of the individual who is manipulative.

As the classroom discussion typically evolves, students come to understand that the differentiation between leadership and manipulation can be somewhat cloudy.

As you begin to construct the façade of your search campaign, it is essential that you become very clear about what guiding principles will define your behaviors in the selection process. It is not my place to tell you what you should or should not do in terms of principled leadership. For your own success, I recommend that you reflect and answer these questions as honestly and directly as you can about your rules of engagement for the selection process:

- Will you represent information in your application, your résumé, and your interviews that is fair, accurate, and sensible?
- Will you present yourself to all you encounter in the search process as genuine, sincere, and appreciative?
- Will you set clear guidelines that determine the consistency and truthfulness of your personal brand and story?

No one can answer these questions for you. The clearer you are about how and why you construct your façade will determine how likely you are to find a job that is consistent and congruent with who you are as a person and as a leader. The consequences for not being clear here can include being discovered as disingenuous or leading you to land a position for which you are not well suited or well matched.

SUMMARIZING AND APPLYING THE JOHARI WINDOW

If you have invested the time, effort, and personal courage to work through the Johari Window exercises, you have a wealth of information that will inevitably inform and improve your opportunities in the selection race. Summarize your major insights so that you can quickly refer to them and think them through as you prepare your résumé, elevator speech, interview strategies, and development plan. In each of the window frames, simply list major bullet points of what you have learned about yourself. An example is provided in Table 5.2. Keep this one-page summary handy as you think through all aspects of your selection preparation and execution.

Update your Johari Window as you move specific insights from quadrant to quadrant. For example, you may discover in your 360 feedback that you have a significant blind spot. If you commit to improving this area and you make it known that you are working on this area with others, it no longer belongs in the blind spots area.

You effectively move this developmental opportunity to the Arena, Frame One. Once a developmental opportunity is in the arena you can actively work on this with the active feedback and support of others around you. Adopt the discipline of reviewing your Johari Window on a monthly basis and add new insights and reassign concepts to various quadrants as you learn and develop.

Taking stock of your strengths and opportunities and filtering this information through the perspective of others can be a challenging task. This process may be particularly daunting in the face of added stress and vulnerability associated with job transition. At the same time, a transition is a remarkable opportunity in which you have both the time and the motivation to develop your self-awareness. Throughout the selection process, all aspects of your style and skills will be thoroughly reviewed and evaluated. It is to your distinct advantage to develop your own understanding of your strengths and opportunities as the basis of shaping the perspective of others.

Table 5.2: An Illustration of a Johari Window

	Known to self	Not known to self
Known to others	Frame One, The Arena: • Extremely results-oriented, gets the job done no matter what. • Quick learner, quickly size people and situations up to make fast decisions. • Strong encourager, provide open and timely feedback to my direct reports.	Frame Two, Blind Spots: • At times, I telegraph that I am uninterested or bored when I am listening to others. • I am sometimes perceived as overly critical of others' ideas. • Occasionally I use my anger as a weapon in the workplace.
Not known to others	Frame Four, The Façade: • Extremely uncomfortable with public speaking. • Fearful that I may be "found out" as inadequate in my new role in the company.	Frame Three, The Unknown: • I successfully figured out our budgeting process with minimal direction after my last promotion. • Quickly defused tension between departments with art of diplomacy and humor.

QUESTIONS FOR REFLECTION

As you complete your Johari Window exercise, consider these questions:

- People have a clear tendency to focus on perceived weaknesses in self-reflection. Have you clearly articulated and acknowledged your strengths as a professional in this exercise? Research suggests that performance is improved to a greater extent by leveraging strengths than attempting to overcome problem areas.
- Blind spots are among the most problematic areas in development as we first must have knowledge of their existence before we can address them. What blind spots were you willing to acknowledge and what are you willing to do to address these areas?
- We all have façades. In many cases it is normal and healthy to keep private parts of ourselves out of the light of day-to-day professional scrutiny. What aspects of yourself are you willing to share openly to select others as the basis of growing?
- What project or opportunity would significantly stretch you beyond your known capacity for performance? Are you willing to commit to this level of challenge to understand the level of work you can achieve? Are failures and setbacks along the way acceptable?
- How will you implement the insights you gain from the Johari Window into your daily work life? What reminders, reinforcers, or people networks can you use to keep you on track?

PART TWO: THE RACE

Part Two is devoted to making the decisions and taking the actions necessary to win the race for selection. Building on our framework of the Olympic hurdles event, Part Two takes you through ten specific hurdles. Each chapter provides key insights, practices, and power strategies that will improve your form, grace, and timing to help you ultimately win the race.

In an Olympic hurdles event, the race begins with a starting gun. The eight runners competing in the final event take their positions at the starting line. At the "on your mark" command, the competitors position themselves in their starting blocks: feet in the blocks; hands behind the line with fingers spread and bridged; one knee on the ground. At the "get set" command they raise their hips, push their feet back against the blocks, and focus their eyes on the first few feet of the track ahead of them. At the sound of the gun, they explode out of the blocks.

In your race for selection, timing is everything. The faster you get out of your blocks, the more speed and momentum you will build. What you accomplish in the first thirty days of your search will inevitably set the pace for the entire race.

The starting sequence for your race will vary based on your situation. In some cases the gun is a sharp and startling bang: the announcement of an organizational reduction of force followed by a sudden meeting with your boss and an HR representative. The starting gun can also be a muffled sound in the distance: the announcement of the acquisition of your company signaling the likelihood of your position being eliminated. In this scenario, your options for the future may be in a state of ambiguity for months.

"Soft starts" in the race for selection can be problematic. Recreational runners in the Boston Marathon may be lined up behind thousands of other runners. It may take a full hour after the starting gun has fired for a person in this position to take off.

In organizational settings where widespread layoffs are anticipated but not scheduled, it's easy to become complacent, hoping against hope that it won't happen to you, thus avoiding the steps necessary to prepare. The bottom line is that it takes a significant amount of time and effort to prepare and start the race for selection. People who make an active decision to get off the mark early will perform significantly better.

The starting gun might also be a signal from an internal impetus for change. You may have been in your position for several years and see little chance for promotion or even lateral moves and feel an increasing detachment and boredom with your job. As this dynamic unfolds, you become increasingly aware that you need to make a move. At some point your comfort with your current role is outweighed by your desire to seek a better challenge. The desire for change may be brought to a head by an unpleasant interaction or outcome. In these cases you will need to pull the trigger on your own if you choose to move forward.

Regardless of the source of the starting gun, as the race begins you have at least three key questions to ask yourself:

1. Am I unwaveringly committed to winning the race as defined by my vision and career objectives?
2. Am I willing to take on the discipline and actions necessary to win the race even if doing so makes me uncomfortable and places me in uncharted waters?
3. Will I create and stick to a plan that will greatly increase the probability and speed of success?

If your answer is a resounding yes to each of these questions, then you are ready to power out of the starting blocks.

PREPARING FOR THE HURDLES

Running a competitive hurdles race starts well before the starting gun. Winning is based on careful planning, the technique and timing of how the runner approaches and clears each hurdle. Every approach, jump, clearing, and landing is scripted to ensure the win.

The following ten chapters of this book outline ten key hurdles that are typically encountered in the race for selection. Your race may include different kinds of hurdles, spaced at different intervals, and you may be running multiple races simultaneously. While these variables make running the selection race significantly different from the highly controlled setting of an Olympic event, the consistent strategy in both events is the planned set up and execution of each hurdle.

With these challenges in mind, these ten chapters focus on key strategies and approaches that mark you as a front-runner from the organization's perspective. Each type of hurdle has its set of "Power Strategies." Based on thorough research and experience, Power Strategies include a brief list of techniques and approaches that will deliver the most improved performance for each hurdle.

CHAPTER SIX
Hurdle One: Building Your Platform

THE BRAVE NEW WORLD OF JOB SOURCING

A few years ago, the title of this chapter might have been, "writing your résumé." In the old days, a job seeker's first interactions with companies and recruiters were built on a continual flow of résumés and cover letters. Those days are over—forever. The new age of job sourcing for organizations and job candidates is here, and it's driven first and foremost by social networking:

- Internal and external recruiters have an extraordinary level of direct access to millions of job candidates through networking sites such as LinkedIn.
- Powerful search engines and applicant tracking tools scrub the web looking for candidates. These searches are based on

sophisticated algorithms that focus on keywords specific to industry and functional requirements.

- Companies are turning their employees into powerful armies of recruiting professionals by offering incentives for qualified referrals.

In this new world, résumés still have an important place, but your interaction with the job search world is far better captured by your platform—the sum total of your message captured by your online profile, résumé, and all your verbal and electronic communications.

If the idea of social networking as a primary way to interface with the job market does not appeal to you, you have a choice. Change your outlook completely or accept that you are virtually eliminating yourself from the competition for a majority of jobs. This is simply a reality in the job sourcing market.

WHAT IS YOUR PLATFORM?

Your selection platform is built on the story of your unique experience, skills, and potential value to a hiring organization. Just like a political campaign, your platform will inform every communication and every document you build as the basis of your successful run.

Hiring decisions are informed by data but are made based on a story. Storytelling is the deepest and most compelling way to convey information. Your story provides the context, the facts, and the motivations that build the flow of meaning for your audience. In a world of ever-increasing speed and flow of communication, your platform must be clear and compelling if it is ever going to make you stand out from your competitors.

To build continuity and power in your job communications, each of these components must be built from the same root story:

- **Your elevator speech:** The initial, compelling statement you use to drive every networking, recruiting, and screening interaction.
- **Your brief bio:** A short summary of your professional experience and career objectives that you will use in general correspondence and web postings.
- **Your social networking profiles:** Your initial message to potential employers and recruiters about your career objectives, your experience, your unique skills, and work history.
- **Your cover letters and e-mail:** All correspondence that you share with recruiters and hiring managers.
- **Your résumé:** The core repository and most detailed expression of your platform.
- **Your interview responses and questions:** The verbal expression of your platform to recruiters and hiring organizations.

Building your platform from the beginning of your race will add significantly to your speed off the starting blocks. Platform construction begins by systematically listing your unique value as illustrated by your past work experience and accomplishments.

THE CHALLENGE, ACTION, RESULTS APPROACH TO PLATFORM DEVELOPMENT

Organizations hire people to get things done. Capturing your ability to accomplish objectives, especially challenging ones, will underscore your core platform messages.

If you accept the premise that the primary purpose of the platform is to tell the story of your unique value as captured by your results in past positions, then consider the Challenge, Action, Results (CAR) approach developed by Robert Meier. Meier is CEO of JobMarketExperts.com, and author of two award-winning books on résumé writing (*The World's Greatest Résumés*, Ten Speed Press, 2005 and *Red Hot Résumés*, Lightspeed Press, 2009). As a past client of Meier's, I can personally speak to the positive impact of his direction in my own career.

Meier's approach is based on his many years of experience in professional résumé writing and his approach can be applied to all aspects of your platform development. His strategies make a significant impact in his clients' ability to gain interviews. The core of Meier's approach is to establish your value proposition in a specific structure that explains results in a clear series of very short, engaging stories. Each story follows this structure:

1. **Challenge:** A brief and compelling description of a business challenge or opportunity in which you led or held a key accountability.
2. **Action:** A statement of the specific strategy and actions you took to achieve the result.
3. **Results:** The actual results your actions achieved supported with meaningful metrics.

The CAR approach sets your accomplishments apart by creating a coherent message that communicates your capabilities and achievements. What CARs leave your fingerprints on the benefits that you delivered for your past employers? Without a distinct connection to you, your results are either questionable or so out of context that they are not impressive.

DEVELOPING YOUR CAR-BASED PLATFORM

Here is a simple process for developing your CAR-based platform:

1. List every job title you have had for the last five to ten years at the top of a separate page of a word processing document (you will want all this information in electronic format, so you can cut and paste it later). If you have had a promotion or a shift in title within the same company, put that on

a separate page. On the left-hand side, write the headings, "Challenge," "Action," "Results," each on separate line, leaving space to write a few sentences after each heading.

2. **Challenges:** Think about all of your experiences in that position. Identify and write down one of the major challenges, major projects, transitions, business events, product launches, or other successful project or organizational opportunity that you have led or significantly supported in that role.

3. **Actions:** Under each challenge, list the specific actions that you took to address that particular challenge. Explain how you decided on those actions. Include an explanation of how you got organizational support, resources, and people aligned and committed to meeting this challenge.

4. **Results:** For every set of actions that you took, list the positive outcomes that were accomplished. Include any specific, measurable impact on the organization.

5. **Repeat:** Repeat this process until you have at least five sets of challenges, actions, results for your last position and two to three for every previous position.

6. **Your unique capabilities:** Finally, review your document. Make a list of all the specific leadership, technical, and problem-solving capabilities you used to achieve these results. Compile these capabilities in a separate list.

Completing this exercise will prepare you for every aspect of your competition moving forward. With these insights in mind, you are ready to start building your key communications.

POWER STRATEGIES FOR USING THE CAR FORMULA

The CAR formula is a different way of thinking about your accomplishments so as to create a compelling story. Here are some additional ideas on driving the process:

1. **Try working backward.** Another way to apply the CAR approach is to outline results first and work backward to the challenge. Think back to your last position and consider the accomplishments you are most proud of that truly distinguish your performance.

2. **Define your results in quantitative terms.** (See the following section on quantifying results on p. 92 for more details.) It's essential to define your success in terms that will be meaningful to your target organization. In many cases that will be linked to dollars, numbers, percentages, or frequencies.

3. **Define your actions in bold declarative terms.** Begin all statements of action with active verbs and focus on actions that you took. If the action was a team effort, acknowledge your collaboration with others and focus on your specific contribution.

4. **Link the challenges to organizational strategy.** Challenges should clearly link to an overarching organizational strategy such as revenue growth, market share, customer base, innovation, etc. The higher the position for which you are applying, the more strategic and wider the scope of the initiative needed.

5. **Begin your platform with your elevator speech.** The first product of your CAR platform should be your elevator speech, a two- or three-sentence statement that captures the key elements of your ability to understand challenges, take actions, and achieve meaningful results specific to the role and organization.

Grounding yourself in the CAR process will make the creation of all other platform documents consistent and cohesive.

BUILDING AND PRACTICING YOUR ELEVATOR SPEECH

A great starting point for expressing your platform is in your elevator speech. In this new world of sound bites and quick connections, your platform message must be clear, compelling, and delivered in thirty to sixty seconds. Your elevator speech must be on the tip of your tongue at all times, and you must deliver it with eloquence and confidence.

Begin by writing out your elevator speech in a specific format. Once you get it nailed, you can easily adapt to specific audiences. There are many frameworks you can use for your elevator speech. The goal is to keep it as simple as possible while still conveying a unique message. Here is a suggested starting point:

1. My name is _____
2. My unique capabilities are _____
3. I am successful at solving this type of challenge _____
4. I consistently achieve these results _____
5. I am looking for this kind of opportunity _____

For example:

1. My name is Dan Charles.
2. I'm a VP of Operations who excels in performance turn-around situations.
3. I have a track record of assessing production, quality, and safety metrics and implementing corrective actions with my management teams within ninety days.
4. I've achieved impressive production improvements with this approach in three plants in the last year resulting in a 24 percent increase in gross margins.

5. I'm looking for a growing manufacturing organization with progressive leadership and a deep commitment to quality systems.

Once you get your elevator speech written, the next step is to tailor it to specific audiences. When you have a specific opportunity in mind, shape your elevator speech to fit the needs or interests of the target organization or networking resource.

Practicing your elevator speech out loud is a great exercise to help you hone your delivery and to begin building your own brand image in your mind. Speaking clearly and succinctly about your strengths and capabilities reinforces your own self-image. Practicing in a mirror or in front a video camera increases your effectiveness as it prepares you for interview delivery.

GET STARTED WITH LINKEDIN

There are a growing number of social networking tools that will form the basis of your networking platform. Start your online platform with LinkedIn. Here are the compelling reasons you should begin with LinkedIn and then build out to other social networking sites and technologies.

- LinkedIn is the largest and most frequently accessed job-networking site in North America.
- LinkedIn is a primary resource for recruiters and web-based data mining applications to access candidates.
- LinkedIn is free and easy to use.

Getting started on LinkedIn is simple. You simply go to the website (Linkedin.com), open an account, and follow the instructions provided. Your initial entries will include:

- Your profile, beginning with your name, your "headline,"

your picture, and a summary of your work qualifications and experiences.

- Your contacts, which include all the people who have some meaningful relationship with you and can provide potential contacts, perspectives, and support in your race for selection.
- Your recommendations, including brief but significant input from individuals who have a solid and positive perspective on your work capabilities. (See section on choosing references in chapter 8, "Hurdle 3.")

There are many approaches to formatting and framing your LinkedIn profile. The best way to get started is to review twenty to thirty profiles of people at your level of management and see what key messages, format, and length you find most compelling and engaging. You'll have the opportunity to build out your elevator speech in clear points that capture the reader's attention.

POWER STRATEGIES FOR BUILDING YOUR LINKEDIN PROFILE

1. **Use LinkedIn daily.** Building your LinkedIn profile and contacts should be a regular part of your day-to-day networking and sourcing activities. Sharpening your profile, adding contacts, and actively networking should be at the core of your profile-building effort.

2. **Focus on quality over quantity of contacts.** Your first impulse on LinkedIn may be to get 500 contacts as quickly as possible. Before you send that invite, ask yourself "Is this person likely to add value to my search or am I likely to add value to this person?"

3. **Keep your updates meaningful.** It's actually preferable to update your LinkedIn profile on a regular basis as your

activities are communicated to everyone in your network. LinkedIn is not Twitter; avoid updates about social activities.

4. **Get engaged in groups.** LinkedIn groups are one of the best ways to connect with people in meaningful exchanges of information, especially in your industry group. Post comments on conversations related to mutual areas of interest. You are also able to connect with group members directly.

5. **Consider advanced features.** The basic subscription to LinkedIn is free. For an upgrade fee, the site offers advanced features specifically for job seekers. These features increase your exposure and your ability to network. You will also get more attention from internal and external recruiters.

A great resource for establishing a strong presence and network within LinkedIn is outlined in the book *The Power Formula for LinkedIn Success: Kick-start Your Business, Brand, and Job Search* by Wayne Breitbarth.

LinkedIn should be the starting point of your platform creation and is only one of dozens of social networking sites and web applications that can be useful to you. Here are three additional approaches you should consider in the early stages of your race:

- **Plaxo.com with Simply Hired:** Plaxo is a professional networking site that is similar to LinkedIn and connects with other social networking tools. Simply Hired is an integrated job search engine that accesses posting information from thousands of job boards and company sites, which can save you considerable time.
- **Blog sites (Blogger, WordPress, etc.):** Blogging is a powerful way to express yourself and network in the job market. If you build out your platform with meaningful commentary and engage in productive discussions, you will likely form solid networking relationships with people with interests related to your professional area.

- **Twitter:** By most accounts, Twitter is a powerful networking tool that enables people to make unique connections. The challenge is that Twitter enables you to share brief pieces of information but not a full profile. It's essential to link your Twitter traffic to your LinkedIn or Plaxo profile for follow up once your connection is established.

The technology and offerings to support social network–based job campaigns is changing rapidly. Additional information on building out your platform through additional sites, blogging, and advanced networking techniques is available at the Million-Dollar Race website (www.TheMillionDollarRace.com).

KEYWORDS IN PROFILES AND RÉSUMÉS

There are many blogs and articles discussing the benefits of keywords in résumés and social networking profiles, and for good reasons. Think of keywords as the search words you use on the Internet. When you have the right search words, your search is going to be more accurate, defined, and efficient. Advanced applicant tracking systems and candidate search tools use the same technology as Internet engines. Recruiters and hiring managers have their own set of keywords for which they instinctively scan as well. The more keywords that are aligned with your industry, level of position, and functional area, the more chances you will be found in a search.

There are many articles and resources available on the web, including recommended keywords for specific searches. The most effective place to start your search for keywords for your résumé and profile is in the job listing for your target position and related job listings. Most organizations begin with the end goal in mind by listing specific keywords in the job posting. The most thorough and useful job postings are typically available on the company website and you should always read these postings in detail when identifying keywords to include in your résumé and profile.

WHAT YOUR RÉSUMÉ AND COVER LETTERS MUST DO

Your résumé must be an extension of your professional platform in a concise, compelling, and completely verifiable document. Each of your competitors has a résumé as well. At some point in the selection process it is likely that your résumé will be compared head-to-head with many other résumés. If you are not competitive in the form, style, clarity, and power of your résumé, you begin the race at a significant disadvantage. Considering the importance and impact of the résumé on the selection process, it's a great place to focus your initial thoughts and energy.

GETTING STARTED: DOING IT YOURSELF OR HIRING A PRO

Chances are that you already have a résumé in hand, especially if you have been in the job market in the past several years. Keep in mind that only the top candidates will ever get the opportunity to interview and that that opportunity may be a result of your résumé.

I believe that professional résumé writers can give you a competitive edge, especially if

- You need to get moving quickly and you're having a hard time pulling it together.
- You don't have ready access to a résumé expert through placement services or a connection to a recruiting professional to support you.
- You don't have the time or inclination to read, research, and distill your own approach to résumé writing.

Given the size of your investment in the job search and the impact on your race, the cost of a professional writer is quite reasonable. If you do your research, read customer reviews, and look specifically for a résumé writer who specializes in senior management to executive clients, you can find a quality provider. Your professional network is a great way to source a qualified service.

USING THE CAR RÉSUMÉ STYLE

The CAR approach to platform development can be applied directly to your résumé as well. Robert Meier's books explain how to build a CAR-based résumé in detail. Consider an example of how the CAR approach can make your résumé content pop.

A candidate for a VP of Finance position had supported the founder and CEO in the successful sale of his company to an investment firm. In a traditional résumé approach, under "experience" for this position, her capabilities were listed as "Provided coordination and leadership for financial planning, budget management, and debt financing while ensuring compliance with standard accounting practices. Led all financial analysis and reporting activities during the due diligence leading up to the sale of the company."

While the description of capabilities is accurate, the compelling story of what the VP accomplished is lost in a list of general accountabilities. Everyone expects a VP of Finance to have these job duties. The key question is, "what is the unique value of this VP to the sale of the corporation?" This is the story that will catch the reader's attention.

Consider this example in the CAR format:

1. **Challenge:** The CEO and board made the determination that the corporation would be sold for maximum sale price within eighteen months.
2. **Action:** Led action team of four analysts to create compelling business case for revenue growth and market share over a five-year horizon.

3. **Results:** The corporation was sold to a private equity firm for $1.2 billion at a debt-to-earnings ratio of 6.5 within twelve months.

Now the story stands out in vivid detail. This VP clearly led a specific course of action, which yielded specific and remarkable business results.

It's valuable to learn other perspectives on résumé styles as well and find an approach that meets your style and needs. The CAR approach is a compelling framework through which to evaluate alternatives. Preparing the CAR approach will also give you a powerful starting point for your interview responses. Learn more about the CAR approach and examples on the Million-Dollar Race website (www.TheMillionDollarRace.com).

QUANTIFYING AND MONETIZING YOUR RESULTS

All résumé books and resources will insist that you capture the results you achieved in clear and measurable terms, preferably with direct financial implications. This is completely true and fairly straightforward for senior leadership, financial, operations, and sales functions where there are direct business metrics associated with performance.

Typical metrics include

- Year over year growth in gross revenues
- Increased margins or total EBITDA
- Budgets managed or total profit and loss accountability
- Increases in productivity
- Bottom line impact of cost or quality initiatives
- Size and speed of acquisitions
- Revenue generated by new product lines

Monetization and qualification of results has become an absolute standard for the senior-level résumé.

So how do you differentiate yourself in response to results? Just increase the figures until they are truly spectacular? Every recruiter and hiring manager has seen countless lists of amazing claims of impact on the business. While numerical data is essential in Results, what will make your performance in the race a standout is the compelling story of *how* you achieved these results in a way that verifies the accomplishment. This means that for every remarkable claim you include in your résumé, you need a CAR response to back it up.

Metrics are also important for functions that are not as directly related to the revenue stream such as Human Resources, Learning, Engineering, and IT leaders. There are key industry standard metrics that drive performance in support of every function and you must be sure your metrics are relevant. Examples of these functional metrics include

- Time and on-budget percentage to implementation
- Percentage of end-user adoption
- Time to hire
- Retention rates
- Customer service ratings

Knowing the industry and the professional literature related to your functional area is the only way to be sure your metrics are meaningful and relevant. Better still, understand the metrics valued by your target company and tie in to those.

OTHER ASPECTS OF YOUR RÉSUMÉ

Once you have the work history of your platform built into your résumé, the remaining elements are straightforward:

- Accurate contact information with confidential phone number and mailing and e-mail addresses
- Career or capability summary, including essential keywords
- Employment history in reverse chronology with all positions

held under a single company heading and dates of employment including month and year

- Education history, including specific degrees earned and certifications
- Professional associations with positions held
- Include community leadership, board memberships, and significant volunteer experiences

Always get several knowledgeable people in your network to review your résumé. If you are not working with a professional writer, be sure your résumé is reviewed by a colleague who regularly evaluates candidates (and is a great proofreader).

COVER LETTERS AND E-MAIL

In a world of information overload and instantaneous communication, the traditional cover or marketing letter is fast becoming a thing of the past. The days of mass mailings of form letters to retained search firms, organizations, private equity firms, and open advertisements are being replaced. LinkedIn profiles, brief networking calls, applicant tracking outputs, and sound bites shared between recruiting professionals is the current state of business.

The time when a cover letter comes into meaningful play is when there is any likelihood that it will be read (i.e., when a personal contact has been established or a direct referral made). In these cases, the cover letter is the introduction to your résumé and should fulfill the following four purposes:

1. Clarify the connection with the reader (referral name or reference to previous conversation).
2. Clearly state the purpose of your inquiry and cite the specific opportunity.
3. Provide a brief (one paragraph) lead-in to résumé with a direct link to an identified need of the organization.

4. Ask for or suggest a next step, follow-up conversation.

That's it. The more brief and to the point your cover letter or e-mail is, the more likely it will be read and elicit a response.

CUSTOMIZING YOUR RÉSUMÉ FOR SPECIFIC OPPORTUNITIES

You will have a standard résumé for networking and search firms. I am often asked if candidates should update their résumés for every application. Not only is it important, it is absolutely vital that you customize your résumé for an ideal job opportunity.

Every organization is looking for a specific solution when they make a significant investment in hiring a senior leader. There is a distinct business need and a compelling strategy behind most hiring decisions. The candidate who is ideally suited and a strong fit for the position will have the career objectives, experience, skills, and passion specifically for that position. If the position is a fit for you, then you have the opportunity to present yourself as an ideal solution. You can't achieve that from a single boilerplate version of your résumé.

POWER STRATEGIES FOR CUSTOMIZING RÉSUMÉS

Customizing individual résumés may seem like a lot of work. If you are organized, it really does not take much time and the benefits far exceed the investment. Here are some useful strategies in managing your custom résumés:

- **Gain control of your résumé.** If you are working with a professional résumé writer, insist from the beginning that your output file will be in a word-processing document that you can edit. The fanciest formatting in the world is of little value if you can't update it or if you have to go back to your résumé writer for updates.

- **Determine your adjustment points.** There are several areas that you can customize to fit a particular opportunity, including career objectives, keywords, specific examples of business outcomes, industry-specific wording or jargon, metrics of interest to a particular organization, and projects and outcomes specifically related to company strategy.

- **Build a file of résumés.** As you begin customizing résumés, save them as separate files with the target company in the filename. If you do this regularly, you'll start building up a repertoire of résumé versions with common themes. This is extremely important if you are applying to organizations in various sectors.

- **Maintain quality control.** Once you start altering résumés, you always open up the possibility of introducing grammatical and formatting errors. If you don't have someone who can do professional-level editing for you, hire somebody on a part-time basis. Unless you are remarkably good at proofing your own materials, get a second pair of eyes.

- **Watch out for "parsing."** If you are submitting a résumé on an organization website (some companies will require you to do this as part of their hiring process), keep in mind that your original document will be "parsed." This means that your résumé will be broken down into component pieces by an automated system. Be sure to check that your résumé was parsed properly before hitting Submit.

Building a repertoire of customized résumés does complicate things. It does, however, have the potential to set you apart and tell your story in a way that has unique meaning for your target organization. Keep close track of your versions by identifying your name and the target organization in the file name to ensure you send the correct version.

CHAPTER SEVEN
Hurdle Two: Sourcing Job Opportunities

How do companies go about hiring people? I asked this question in interviews with people who design and direct applicant-tracking software and application process, including Lance Brolin, who has managed recruiting operations for Fortune 500 companies. Recruiters and recruiting processes are highly consistent and predictable in most mid- to large-sized organizations:

1. Hiring managers fill out a job requisition, get budget approval, and forward the requisition to the recruiting department.
2. Recruiting managers decide how to post the position and whether to use an external agency.
3. Recruiting managers usually review candidates in this order of priority:
   - Internal candidates
   - Networking and employee referrals

- Recruiting agency referrals
- Direct application through company recruiting website or job boards. This may include sorting through hundreds of applications, of which 75 percent are unqualified.

Recruiters are very busy people and typically have a large number of positions to fill quickly. Digging through résumés and applications takes a great deal of time and energy, even if the process is automated. Any time a candidate comes to the attention of the recruiter through a network connection or an employee referral there is a far greater chance that the recruiter is going to take the time to review that candidate's résumé.

With this reality in mind, it is clear that a referral is by far your best chance at getting in the door of any organization. Accordingly, your job-sourcing activities should therefore break down in this division of time and effort:

- 80 percent: networking
- 15 percent: agency contacts
- 5 percent: direct application and job boards

The exception to this rule is for senior executive positions, which are often controlled by retained searches. The higher the level and scope of the position, the more professional recruiters will be involved. This means you should spend far more of your days making contacts, doing company research, and working on your network profile than filling out applications.

NETWORKING IS ALSO A NUMBERS GAME

While social networking demands a strong set of skills and drive, the activity is also a numbers game. You have a circle of network contacts; your contacts have their circle, and so forth. By tapping into other networks, you gain access to exponentially more people and have a larger pool of resources. This is the basis of all social network sites: your two hundred contacts may draw a second order of thirty thousand contacts and a third order over of two million. There are few people in the world of business who cannot be accessed through effective networking.

Building your network and sourcing job opportunities will likely be the core activity of your race for some time before you begin making specific contacts and setting up initial interviews. It is crucial that you commit a specific amount of time every day (typically two or three hours) to sourcing activities and that you set specific goals for each of three principal networking activities:

1. **Making contacts:** Reaching out to network connections, recruiters, and potential organizations with an e-mail, social networking connection, or phone call. Contact activities should be brief interactions focused on arrangements for more extended meetings.
2. **Setting meetings:** Having extended phone conversations or face-to-face interactions regarding your job campaign.
3. **Landing interviews:** All successful networking activities will eventually lead to some sort of formal or informal interview process in which your candidacy and fit for a particular job will be assessed.

Each level of activity drives results in the next category. Experienced sales professionals understand the simple numbers game involved in building their pipelines and getting sales. The same applies for getting interviews: Twenty contacts a day may lead to five meetings per week, which may lead to two interviews per month.

If your goal is to have four interviews per month, then it would be best to begin your pace at forty contacts per day using this formula.

This approach requires a specific discipline and schedule and is best tracked using some system for recording contacts and follow-up notes. It's particularly challenging to maintain this pace once you begin the process of interviewing and traveling for meetings, so the most successful competitors block out a specific period of time each day in which they will commit without fail to sourcing activities. There is a complete activity tracking template available on the Million-Dollar Race website (www.TheMillionDollarRace.com).

Even when particular job leads look promising, there is no value in backing off on sourcing activities. Both internal and external recruiters are keenly aware of the job candidate's motivation level. Activity and contacts that are not maintained tend to cool off quickly.

THE FAILURE OF JOB BOARDS: THEIR SUCCESS

With the advent of the Internet age, the promise of job boards proved to be a game-changing resource in the job market. Removing the expense, timing, and location limitations of print advertising, organizations can now post their jobs in a way that can be viewed by limitless numbers of potential candidates. At the same time, job candidates can access tens of thousands of job searches instantaneously using advanced search techniques. In theory, this technological advancement would greatly enhance the opportunity for ideal candidates to find their ideal job opportunities.

Unfortunately, job boards have proven to be so effective at communicating job opportunities that the online recruitment and selection processes have consistently been overrun with applications. In many cases, high-value job opportunities can attract over five thousand applications, the vast majority of these from unqualified candidates. This onslaught has resulted in organizations being far more selective in their recruitment and selection procedures by placing more filters on application inflows and placing more emphasis on alternative sourcing techniques such as social networking and internal job referrals.

Don't jump to the conclusion, however, that job boards are useless in providing any value in the competitive job sourcing process.

In fact job boards, especially niche job boards that serve specific functional areas, high salary ranges, and geographies provide a wealth of information about the job market in general, insights into hiring organizations, and the latest trends in staffing and job descriptions. Job boards are simply not an efficient or effective means of initiating a non-orchestrated job sourcing campaign. Using job boards and organizational career sites exclusively can give you the false sense of security when, in fact, you may be missing the best opportunities.

AVOID FEAR-BASED RÉSUMÉ SPAMMING

Perhaps the least effective and potentially time-wasting activity with which to begin your job sourcing activities is a blind spraying of the Internet with your résumé. This knee-jerk reaction is typical of job candidates who do not have better coaching or superior job sourcing skills. Résumé spamming is a poor way to approach the job sourcing process for these three reasons:

1. It reinforces a mindset of desperation wherein you are casting about aimlessly hoping for a lucky break. It distracts you from the competitive perspective from which you control the race.
2. Once your résumé has been listed on a job board, you lose complete control of how it will be communicated, who will read it, and your ability to update or change the information based on a specific opportunity.
3. You are guaranteeing an entrée into a job-selection process that puts you head-to-head with tens of thousands of other job candidates.

Your objective is to enter only into the races that have a high likelihood of leading to a position aligned with your objectives. Why would you invest precious time on efforts that are not focused on that goal?

NETWORKING: THE ULTIMATE KEY TO JOB SOURCING SUCCESS

There is no skill or activity that approaches the importance or effectiveness of networking in your ability to source the best job opportunities. There are three key trends in the current job market that should help you understand and appreciate the power of networking:

1. **The hidden job market:** By some reports, 80 percent of positions filled are never listed in the open job market. The only way that you can access the vast majority of job opportunities is through the network of people you know and the people they know who can connect you with these "hidden" opportunities.

2. **The power of recommendations:** One of the primary ways in which you differentiate yourself from the vast sea of nameless résumés that typically surround a high-value job opportunity is the personal reference of someone you know. Recruiters and hiring managers are far more likely to follow up on a lead based on a personal recommendation from someone they know and trust.

3. **The rise of social networking:** Powerful online services, such as LinkedIn, Facebook, and Twitter, provide fast and effective means to establish meaningful connections with people who will connect you with opportunities. Organizations and recruiters are turning to these tools in ever increasing numbers to source qualified candidates.

These trends should lead you to the conclusion that a robust job sourcing process begins with networking and builds out to other sources, including job boards, recruiters, and outplacement services.

BUILDING YOUR BASE FOR NETWORKING

The power of networking is driven by two key aspects of social behavior that are present in all business interactions. The first is the genuine desire that most people have to help others. People like to help others; it helps them feel competent, capable, and powerful, and it leads to the likelihood that they will also benefit from the interaction, even if not directly or immediately. The power of helping others without expectation of immediate reward is a core message of many sales and leadership philosophies.

The second powerful driver of networking behavior is reciprocation. People have a natural tendency to share information and resources, and there is a natural expectation that their helpful behaviors will be reciprocated in the future. This means that a core part of the networking process includes a focus on the needs and motivations of the people with whom you network. People who network expecting to focus only on their needs and outcomes will quickly burn through valuable relationships.

Successful networkers understand this dynamic and always build in some opportunity for reciprocal action, even if it is simply a follow-up note and an ongoing update on how the networking information was used or provided value.

GET STARTED WITH YOUR CORE TEAM

Everyone has sources of network connections. Begin building your initial network list from the following sources:

- Your family and friends (review your phone and e-mail directory)
- Your current or previous work colleagues for at least the past seven years

- Your close business networking connections
- Schoolmates

From all of these network connections, choose the top twenty to thirty contacts with whom you have a meaningful connection and feel comfortable contacting. This will form your "core team," the people who are going to build the foundation of your network and will be cheering you on from the stands. These are the people who are most likely going to refer you to other people, resources, and opportunities.

You only have one chance to make your first impression and request of this all-important team. Be fully prepared to make the most of your initial conversations. A great way to prepare is to have an outline of the key points you want to make in a brief networking call:

- Extend a warm greeting and reinforce your connection with your contact.
- Briefly state the reason for your call (avoid lengthy explanation of your current situation).
- Provide a very brief and specific overview of the type of organization and position for which you are looking.
- Request a referral to any opportunities or particular organizations that might fit your profile.
- Always ask for additional contacts to add to your network and if it's OK to mention their name and contact.

The last point is the most important aspect of your network building. The essence of building your networking base is building out new connections. Any network conversation that does not end with referrals or connections is a dead-end.

Once you've built your core team, make a commitment to be in contact with them at least monthly to provide them with updates on your search. This will keep you in the forefront of their mind and will help them feel part of your winning team.

POWER STRATEGIES FOR NETWORKING

One of the most important aspects of networking is to recognize that while people are willing to help, business people tend to be extraordinarily busy, with limited time and resources for activities that are not directly related to their jobs. Strong networkers appreciate this fact and follow these power strategies of networking:

- **Be prepared.** Do not begin networking until you are precisely clear on your career focus, ideal position description, and preferred organization. Networking should be used as an opportunity to zero in on opportunities emanating from your clarity of vision, not for ad hoc career counseling.
- **Track your activities.** Networking should emerge from a specific plan of action, which includes carefully recording networking contacts, information discussed, follow-up actions, and making a commitment to follow through with the network contact.
- **Get to the point.** Be prepared to ask for exactly what you want in a network interaction. Few things are more frustrating for an individual volunteering their time than for you to go on about your professional story without getting to the specific information or contacts you are seeking.
- **Follow up, relentlessly.** Marketing professionals know it takes five to seven contacts with the consumer to influence a buying decision. Regular updates and connections with your network will sustain their conscious efforts to support your search.
- **Reciprocate.** Always ask and listen for the needs and interests of your network contact. They may not be looking for a job, but they may value a business contact, the sales lead, or even a good article or link related to an area of interest.

It's easy to forget how busy people are; the more concise, clear, and compelling your communication in networking, the better.

The Power of Serendipity in Networking

You don't need to be deeply spiritual or have a profound faith in the divine order of the universe to recognize the power of serendipity in life events. Every once in a while, things do just work out in a way that seems ideal and situations change quickly against all odds. In an active and vibrant networking process, people show up, connections are made, and old relationships are reignited. Every time your story is shared in a memorable and provocative way, it gets repeated to others.

I shared my goals and objectives in a breakfast meeting with a close colleague. Within two weeks that colleague was literally running through the airport attempting to catch a plane and saw a neighbor who was also VP of human resources for a local company. In thirty seconds of a passing conversation, the VP asked my friend if he had any contacts that could help them with succession planning.

Within two weeks, I was sitting down with the VP and the CEO of this corporation explaining how I could help them put together a successful succession planning and leadership development program. When the VP shared that they did not have the internal resources to accomplish this project, the conversation quickly turned to a full-time job. As a result, I earned a full-time, high-paying position with an office twelve minutes from my home, which lasted two and a half years.

Whether you view this outcome as divine providence or natural occurrence generated by the sheer probability of contacts through networking, there is profound potential for networking to generate unanticipated results. And that may be all you need to move on.

THE BEST JOB-SOURCING TOOL EVER: THE INFORMATIONAL INTERVIEW

Over the years I have given and received hundreds of hints and best practices on the most effective ways to build networks. Of all the techniques that I've used, by far the most successful in getting an inside perspective on an organization (or just about any topic for that matter) is the informational interview. Informational interviews can open up many job searches and have, in many cases, led directly or through a referral to a job opportunity.

An informational interview is a brief (less than twenty minutes) call or face-to-face meeting in which you ask an individual who works for a target organization for a brief overview of their experience and perception of the organization. I would estimate that the success rate of this technique is well over 90 percent based on the consistently enthusiastic response I hear from people who use this approach.

The main reason why the informational interview works so well is that most people talk readily about themselves and their experiences, so long as you are not asking them for anything particular in return (e.g., ask for sale, a personal referral, recommendation, etc.) and you agree that the conversation is completely confidential. Once people understand that their views and opinions are the main topic of the discussion and that they are truly helping another individual, they're delighted to talk openly.

HOW TO CONDUCT AN INFORMATIONAL INTERVIEW

The purpose of an informational interview is for you to get a candid, open, and frank perspective on the organizational culture and what it's like to work in that culture from an individual perspective.

To initiate an informational interview follow these simple steps:

1. As you are doing organizational research, use LinkedIn, professional groups, or other social networking opportunities to get a referral for the name of an individual who works within your target organization.
2. Once you've selected an individual, call or e-mail them, state the purpose of your inquiry, and see if you can arrange a

time to talk. Calling will typically yield a better hit rate than e-mail. Begin by stating the name of a person or source who referred you or a meaningful connection and ask for no more than twenty minutes of their time.

3. Once you've arranged for a time, explain to your contact that you would like to have a brief conversation regarding their experience and perceptions of the organization. You should be prepared with at least three to five open-ended questions that center on the things that you find most important about culture, structure, or their specific job in their organization.

4. As a matter of professional courtesy, always call your contact immediately at the time scheduled, and ask "Is this still a good time to talk?" This conveys that you recognize that the informational interview is not a top priority for the individual.

5. Conduct the informational interview, taking notes on your contact's responses. As the informational interview can easily run long, make sure that you do not go over the amount of time that you contracted. If you acknowledge the time, your contact may invite you to stay on longer or may engage you in questions about your own career search. This often leads to interesting leads or other network connections.

6. Always write a thank-you note within twenty-four hours of your contact. An e-mail note would suffice, but a written thank-you note sent by snail mail will make a lasting impression and reflect your true appreciation.

The results of the successful informational interview can be astounding. I've often heard of job candidates being referred to others or being told that there is an unlisted search going on within their organization and who to contact. Always remember the power of reciprocation and offer any insights, suggestions, or useful information to your contact in addition to a thoughtful thank-you note.

GETTING THE MOST OUT OF OUTPLACEMENT SERVICES

If you are being terminated from a full-time position in a mid- to large-sized organization due to acquisition or other downsizing initiative, you are likely to get outplacement services and a severance package. By all means you should avail yourself of this offer and not attempt to negotiate more severance pay in lieu of receiving the services.

Large and well-established outplacement services have a remarkable number of resources that can turbocharge the beginning of your job search, including placement, résumé support, interview training, temporary office space, and guided support groups. Some outplacement firms also offer sophisticated, proprietary online search support services for doing organizational research that are not available to the general public.

Most outplacement firms are driven by a business model to serve as many clients as possible at a fixed cost per client. This means that many of their services are offered à la carte and it's up to the initiative of the job candidate to fully utilize the services available. Outplacement firms are also focused on "teaching you to fish" rather than doing the fishing for you. Develop a strong relationship with your outplacement contact and consistently ask for specific support. If you can arrange for weekly or biweekly meetings to review your job search progress, do so. It is less likely that you will get this level of attention and support unless you specially ask for it.

WORKING WITH RECRUITERS AND RECRUITING FIRMS

Imagine if you had a team of individuals with outstanding network connections who stayed up nights thinking of ways to connect you with an ideal job. The fantastic news is that this is exactly the life-blood of professional recruiters and recruiting firms. The challenge is that working with professional recruiting firms is every bit as competitive and complex as is working directly with organizations and internal recruiters.

As with every hurdle in the selection race, working with professional recruiters requires thoughtful planning and careful execution. Before you begin sourcing and contacting search professionals, learn how search firms work and what their business interests are in working with job candidates. There are three basic realities you need to take into account before you engage with a recruiting professional or firm.

Reality 1: Recruiting Firms Work for the Hiring Organization

Recruiting firms are paid by the hiring organization. Their business priorities and actions are determined by the needs and expectations of their paying clients. This doesn't mean that professional recruiters are not caring, thoughtful, and ethical business people. It just means that, at the end of the day, your value to recruiters is determined by your potential to be the candidate of choice.

Implications for You

Regardless of how genuine, caring, and supportive your recruiting professional is, you must watch out for your own needs. Don't allow yourself to be swayed by their enthusiasm. Keep yourself grounded in what *you* want.

Reality 2: Recruiting Firms Provide Great Value and Charge a Lot of Money

Companies consistently engage recruiting firms because they offer a great value. Tracking down, sourcing, and qualifying candidates takes an enormous amount of time and resources. Most companies offering high-paying jobs are willing to invest a significant amount to outsource this service. As a general rule, the fee for a successful search will range between 25 percent and 35 percent of the first year of the candidate's salary. That fee is set once you are formally introduced to a firm by a recruiting company.

Implications for You

The moment you are represented by a recruiting firm, your potential hiring organization is going to be socked with a significant premium to pay to employ you. If you are looking at a $200,000 per year position, you are now $50,000 to $70,000 more expensive to a hiring organization. Is this terrible? The answer is "absolutely not," *if* you are the right candidate *and* the recruiter gets you into a new opportunity. It's merely a potential plus if you make the connection without the agency.

Reality 3: Contingency Search and Retained Search Are Different Business Models

Before you engage with a search firm or professional, you must understand the differences between these two kinds of contracted searches.

Contingent search

Recruiting firms are paid only when they successfully place a candidate (typically when they start). Contingent search firms have a clear business strategy: find the best candidates possible and represent them to as many companies as possible. Typically a contingent search will only represent you to the firms and opportunities that they approve with you. If they think you are a hot prospect, they will be pitching you to many opportunities.

Implications for You

Contingency search firms identify candidates for a great number of potential companies. They don't stand to make any money unless they successfully make a connection that ends in a hire. Provided you interview well, they are absolutely delighted to have you interview with as many companies as possible.

Be prepared to be told that you are a "unique" candidate and that they have "just the right opportunity" for you. While that might feel like a great opportunity to get your search moving, remember that every interview process that is not a good fit for you is a waste of time for you, the recruiting professional, and the hiring organization.

Retained Search

In a retained search, the recruiting firm is contracted to fill a particular position. Retained search firms are typically paid in three installments as candidates are sourced, slated, and selected by the hiring organization. In this case, the recruiting firm is far more interested in representing a carefully selected slate of candidates who are fully prepared. Retained searches are far more exclusive, involve fewer candidates, and may offer a superior representation to the hiring companies.

Implications for You

Both retained and contingent firms vary in terms of reputation and influence with the hiring organization. Retained search firms and retained search processes are considered by hiring organizations to be of higher caliber and more prestigious (such considerations justify the fact that the organization is putting the money up front). Retained searches are also used more frequently for senior executive–level positions.

The great advantage for the candidate in working with a professional recruiting firm is that there should never be a fee. All fees and expenses, including travel, are charged directly to the client organization. Search firms that charge a retainer to the candidate should be avoided at all costs.

The challenge of working with a search firm is to remember that their continued business with a hiring organization is completely contingent upon the quality of candidates they present and the eventual success of the candidates that they place within that organization. One unsuccessful placement could result in a significant loss of revenue for the individual or the firm. That said, your interaction with a search firm should be every bit as calculated, focused, and executed as any direct interaction with a hiring organization.

POWER STRATEGIES FOR WORKING WITH RECRUITERS

As you research and network to identify professional recruiters or recruiting firms keep in mind these important strategies:

- Search firms are always interested in new candidates if the candidates are highly qualified and would effectively represent the firm to the hiring organization. Your initial impression and level of interest will make a significant difference in the recruiter's motivation to work with you.
- Search firms are just as blanketed with e-mails, cover letters, and résumés as any hiring organization. Using networks and personal introductions to search professionals is essential if you plan to stand out in any way. Cold-calling search firms, particularly large firms, is typically regarded as a nuisance.
- Search firms come in all different sizes, industry-specific segments, and tend to focus on specific pay ranges. Large recruiting firms tend to have a great deal more reach and clout in the job market, while smaller, boutique firms, and individual recruiters tend to have more time and energy to focus on the individual needs of the job candidate. A solid race plan includes all sizes of search firms.

- Most recruiters are highly professional business people with a sincere interest in helping people connect with an ideal organization. At the same time, they are extremely busy and pulled by many competing agendas. Don't take it personally if your calls are not returned immediately or you feel you are not their top priority in the moment.
- Search firms will screen you as a candidate in much the same way hiring organizations do. The chapter on screening interviews will be very helpful to review prior to your first conversation with a recruiting professional.

Keep in mind that recruiters will reflect your energy, enthusiasm, and openness to job opportunities to potential hiring organizations. Anything that you convey to a recruiter as a potential barrier to pursuing a job opportunity will quickly move you away from the top of their list. Professional recruiters make money when they place people. Making that as easy as possible for them will ensure you get the greatest attention and commitment.

WHAT ABOUT CONSULTING?

Consulting assignments are an outstanding opportunity to get reestablished in a challenging job market. There are several factors in our evolving job market that make consulting a great opportunity for job candidates:

- As companies grow, they're looking to build work capacity without increasing full-time headcount, which includes the expenses of a full benefits package. Hiring consultants allows for flexible growth while managing overhead.
- There are a growing number of firms that represent professionals and mid-level managers on a contract-to-hire basis and will pleased to represent you to firms. This gives you and the hiring

organization the opportunity to "test drive" the relationship, which can be a real bonus.

- Consulting assignments can add a great deal of structure and sense of accomplishment to your workday. This can be extremely helpful in establishing your sense of self-esteem as well as providing a great explanation of what you are doing in your transition.

- Many individuals successfully transferred their professional lives into full-time, independent or boutique firm consulting careers that have added a great deal of meaning, flexibility, and, eventually, a solid income.

An individual in a race for selection should always be open to opportunities for short-term consulting contracts, particularly if the search is likely to go over three months. At the same time, taking on consulting work during the job sourcing process can also introduce complications.

POWER STRATEGIES FOR MANAGING CONSULTING THROUGH YOUR TRANSITION

- As you build your platform and work through your networking opportunities, be very clear if you are committed to finding a full-time position *or* if you are committed to full-time consulting. Companies are more reluctant to hire you as a consultant, particularly in long-term assignments, if they believe you are likely to leave as soon as you get a job.

- Consulting assignments are fantastic for bridging financial needs, but they will also cut into the time, energy, and focus you have for finding a full-time position. A common phenomenon is for people to become comfortable with the level of consulting work that keeps them moving but it takes the drive out of their sourcing campaign for a full-time position.

- Making a commitment to being a full-time consult is a significant shift. For most people making the transition, the greatest challenge is building an effective business development process, including sales and marketing channels. This can be extremely expensive and time-consuming to establish, particularly if you are not naturally comfortable with sales.
- Networking with other consultants is a great way to build capacity and potentially take online larger assignments. If you plan to do this on a short-term basis, it is best to have a solid letter agreement regarding business development, ownership of intellectual property, and sales commissions for bringing in new clients. Committing to long-term partnership agreements, forming a corporation, or investing a great deal of money in sales and marketing initiatives may not make sense if your commitment is to find a full-time position.
- There are typically a great number of consulting positions for talented and committed professionals in the large consulting companies. These positions include solid pay and a great opportunity to build networks. At the same time, these positions typically demand sixty to eighty hours of work per week and include extensive travel requirements.

There's no question that consulting can be an outstanding opportunity to work through a job transition. Your key challenge in sourcing and taking on consulting assignments is to ensure that the opportunities work for you and take you where you want to be professionally.

Networking is what you make of it. If you see it as a mindless chore, you'll convey that level of engagement (or lack thereof) in your communications. If you see it as a healthy adventure that is opening you to new people and opportunities, you will bring that level of energy and commitment to the process.

In either case, you need to set a discipline and time commitment to networking activities every day. Most skilled networkers can do this in less than two or three hours per day provided they are consistent in their approach. As long as the contact, meeting, and interview ratios are meeting your targeted expectations, there is no need to invest excessive time in networking.

The true results of networking are only developed and appreciated over time. Your network is a living organism. If you feed it and develop it on an ongoing basis, it will naturally grow and unfold in ways you cannot predict. The broader and more vibrant your network is, the greater the number of opportunities in which you will come into contact. Each of the opportunities that offer potential fit and promise for you also need your consistent attention. With practice, consistency, and follow-through, networking will become an integral part of your professional life.

CHAPTER EIGHT
Hurdle Three: References and Background Checks

THE DRIVE FOR VERIFICATION

The million-dollar job is a high-stakes proposition. There is a natural tendency for job candidates to present themselves in the best light possible. The difference between getting a job and not getting a job greatly impacts long-term financial stability, retirement, and the ability to maintain the lifestyle to which mid- and upper-level professionals have become accustomed. Given this enormous pressure, people will always err on the side of sharing positives with the perspective employer.

All organizations and recruiting professionals recognize this fundamental tendency and have developed elaborate and sophisticated means for verifying information shared by job candidates. Two primary vehicles for validating the history and accomplishments of job candidates include job references and background checks. Before extending an offer to any job candidate, there is typically a careful and thoughtful review of both sources of information. Poor information from either source can quickly undermine even the most promising job interviews.

Begin your job search with these two important aspects of the verification hurdle in mind. The more you understand about the dynamics, potential, and influence of these critical aspects of your job campaign, the better prepared you will be to clear this hurdle. Both challenges should be addressed in the early stages of your planning.

Cleaning Up Your Google Footprint

The moment you make a network connection in the emerging web environment, you are likely to trigger two events: people will either Google your name or look up your LinkedIn profile. In the former case, all information that you have ever offered to the web will appear, including any social media connections, news items or write-ups, previous employment links, as well as every blog post or online review you ever created. If you have a common name, you are likely to be covered by the cloak of anonymity. If not, it's worth checking to see what is there and taking the following actions as needed:

- Delete any social networking accounts if you are not actively using or updating them.
- Write to webmasters of old employment sites and request that they remove references to you if they are not current.
- Delete any controversial posts, reviews, comments that portray you as angry, politically extreme, or inappropriate.
- Clean up your Facebook or any other network account, removing any pictures or posts you would not joyfully share with a future employer.
- Consider posting and blogging on industry-related sites with insightful and well-written comments. These will eventually push to the top of a Google search and be the first items a potential employer sees.

There is more you can do if you encounter problems or issues, including services that can help you with clean ups. Just Google, "clean up my Google footprint" for great articles and posts on the subject.

CHOOSING REFERENCES WISELY

Professional references are one of the most time-honored and revered resources in verifying qualification for selection. In the days before mass communication, a written letter of recommendation could quickly open doors to trade, business deals, and even loan agreements based solely on the credibility and reputation of the endorser. While the focus and centrality of references may have lost some mystique in an era of fast-paced, virtual communication, the job reference continues to be a deciding factor in most executive-level hiring decisions.

It's a solid, competitive practice always to be consciously thinking about who your references might be, what aspects and perspectives they are likely to share about you, and how their credibility and background would be perceived by a potential employer.

POWER STRATEGIES FOR BUILDING REFERENCES

As you think about choosing your references for your job search, consider these core strategies.

- **Choose people who know your work.** Include individuals who have firsthand knowledge of your leadership skills and accomplishments based on regular and consistent interaction. Not all of your references need to be work colleagues or bosses, but it is essential to include at least three or four who have worked with you on a regular day-to-day basis.
- **Build diversity.** It's great to have one or two CEOs or board members in your reference list. It is also useful to have peers, direct reports, and even clients or customers if they have a long-term working relationship with you and can speak to specifics of your abilities.

- **Verify ability and willingness.** Are your references willing and able to share information with potential employers freely and openly? Some organizations have policies restricting information to be shared in references.
- **Consider availability.** With some individuals' work schedules it's difficult to schedule an appointment. A reference from someone who is not easily accessible or responsive will do little to help your cause.
- **Do not ask for written letters initially.** The days of letters of recommendation as standard operating procedure in the selection process are over. Do not request this time-consuming activity up front, unless you know it's required for a specific opportunity. Willing references offer more value by writing a brief recommendation on LinkedIn. Most hiring organizations are now calling references directly.

With these considerations in mind, it's best to source four to seven references, at least two for every full-time position you have had in the past ten years. Your hiring organization may only ask for three or four references. It's better to have a variety of references to draw on, depending on the specific opportunity for which you are being considered. If you are conducting multiple searches at the same time, it may be helpful to spread out a number of references to avoid any individual being called multiple times within a short period.

THE ART OF ENGAGING REFERENCES

In an old-school business tradition, asking for and receiving references in the form of letters of recommendation was a top-down and highly covert interaction. A subordinate in an organization would deferentially approach a superior and ask for a letter of recommendation without any question as to its quality or key indications. The actual letters and summary conclusions of the writer were never shared or discussed with the job candidate, and tradition dictated that the hiring organization would never share this information with a candidate as well.

Some of this staid perspective still hangs on, particularly within traditional corporate cultures, and is more typical of business leaders with many years of experience. It's important that you respect this mindset when approaching your references. It's also best only to engage references with whom you can have an open conversation about the intent of your job campaign and a clear understanding of the reference's motivation and perspective on serving as a reference.

POWER STRATEGIES FOR RECRUITING REFERENCES

When approaching references it's helpful to keep these five specific guidelines in mind:

1. Be open and candid about your career search and objectives. References can be most helpful to you if they have a full understanding of your ideal career goals. The more articulate and specific you can be, the more helpful they can be in supporting your intentions.

2. Ask candidates if they are fully able and available to serve as references. A great starting point would be to ask them to provide a brief LinkedIn reference. Any indication of lack of time may suggest that a reference has other reservations and may not be the best source. It's better to provide an easy out than to pressure a reluctant reference.

3. Give your references some key highlights or accomplishments you think would be useful in illustrating your capability should they be contacted. If they're truly your advocate, they will appreciate the suggestion. Be sure they have an up-to-date copy of your résumé.

4. Your references will most likely be asked the question, "What

do you see as this candidate's weaknesses or opportunities for development?" They may also be asked the reason you're leaving your current position. Have an open discussion with references on each of these topics.

5. Think carefully about how you approach references if your job search is confidential. By sharing your intent with people in your current company or associated customers or vendors, you potentially put them and yourself at odds with the goals in your current role. It may be preferable to approach potential references only after your intent to depart is publicly known.

Selecting and preparing a strong list of references is a time-consuming process. It may not seem like an immediate priority as you prepare for the race. Consider that the people you choose as job references may be the strongest advocates for you and your future endeavors. These conversations will likely lead to the building of your networking contacts.

The efforts that you invest in building your team of references will also build your close allies and supporters, those who will be cheering from the sidelines as you run the race. Stay in close contact with your references throughout your campaign to be sure that they are updated and prepared should they receive that all-important call.

BACKGROUND CHECKS

In an age of extraordinary access to information, including personal information, background checks have become a standard protocol for most hiring organizations. In situations where there are multiple qualified candidates to consider, background checks can help an organization quickly identify candidates who have undesirable backgrounds or who were less than candid in the information they shared in their résumé, application, or interviews.

Negative or disparate news in the background check can quickly kill a hiring decision. You should fully understand the scope and purpose of the background check before making an application for a position. Full background checks for mid- to senior-level leadership positions are typically initiated as a final slate of candidates is identified by the hiring organization and completed prior to final interviews.

Background checks are typically completed by third-party vendors who specialize in the sourcing of information and the intensive follow-up involved in a standard review process. The cost of these background checks is very reasonable. Organizations want to be sure candidates pass their background check before flying them in for an interview.

So what is involved in the background check and what should you be aware of as a job candidate? I had the opportunity to conduct an informational interview with Jon White, Strategic Accounts Manager, at Aurico, a leading provider of employment background checks for large organizations. He shared some key aspects of the background checking process:

- When you are actively interviewing with a company that uses an outside provider to conduct a background check, you will be asked to sign a disclosure and consent that gives the company permission to contract with a verification and background check provider. This disclosure and authorization form will spell out all the areas in which that organization can legally collect information about you.
- The focus of background checks may vary, but they most commonly include court-related criminal investigations or convictions, driver history, credit reports (financial related positions), employment verification, and educational verification. Special searches can also consider professional certification or licensure.
- The use of background checks is regulated by the Fair Credit and Reporting Act and is further directed by individual state laws.
- Thorough criminal background checks are conducted based

on an investigation of all counties where you have lived or worked. The number of years would vary based on job category or industry (e.g., health care or child care), but a typical check encompasses the past seven years. Each county court is contacted to determine if you have criminal records.

· Employment and educational verification is conducted either through established databases that maintain your record from a school or an employer or by contacting previous employers and schools you have listed.

Given the consistent application and rigor of background checks in the job market, you should be aware and prepared should any negative information emerge (e.g., major misdemeanor records and felony records). Another potential consideration is a poor credit report. An organization needs to have a clear reason to preclude a person from a position based on a credit report, usually based on direct fiduciary responsibilities. In some cases use of credit reporting is restricted by state law.

Should any negative information be reported that has a bearing on the employment decision, the job candidate has the right to review the background report and dispute any inaccurate information. Should you lie awake at night worrying about that underage drinking charge you got in college? Probably not. Most hiring organizations are willing to overlook minor infractions or issues unless there is a pattern of repeated offense.

Should you have an incident or an exception that may appear on your background check, it's best that you manage the communication proactively by approaching your primary contact within the hiring organization before the formal interview process. If the issue is one that would have a direct bearing on your employability, it would be far better to address this up front. Having damaging information come to light leaves you open to the potential inference that you were trying to cover this up. In general, people are more tolerant of past mistakes from which a clear lesson has been learned than they are of individuals who have not been forthcoming. Given the thoroughness and rigor behind the modern background check, honesty is the best policy.

CHAPTER NINE
Hurdle Four: The Screening Interview

Screening interviews, which are preliminary to the full interview process, include interactions with search professionals, HR staff, internal and external recruiters, or, in rare cases, the hiring manager. These interviews are typically no longer than thirty minutes and are often framed as "an opportunity to get to know you."

Screening interviews are, in most cases, well orchestrated and carefully evaluated exercises designed to quickly narrow the selection. This means that the screening interview is often loaded with questions designed to end the process quickly if you do not have the right answer.

When preparing for screening interviews for a job that fully meets your career objectives, your primary objective is to make it through the screening so that you have the chance to explore the job further. Anything you say or ask for in this interview that would raise flags or plant seeds of doubt about your candidacy will not serve you.

There are a few key considerations to keep in mind as you prepare for a screening interview.

The person conducting the screening interview is most likely not directly involved in the final hiring decision. They will make a recommendation to the hiring manager or committee based on preset criteria and the general "sense" of you as a candidate. If the person conducting the initial interview is a more junior search professional or HR generalist, they may be eager to demonstrate their effectiveness by erring on the side of exclusion. For you, this means answering all the interview questions with a positive and enthusiastic manner. Discerning questions on your part can be directed in the main interview process to people who are more knowledgeable about the position and with whom you've established a clear rapport.

Screening interviewers will typically be asked what strengths and weaknesses they see in the candidate, and they may be required to report their observations in writing. This means that a screening interviewer will be actively looking for shortcomings to fill in that blank. A skillful interviewee is aware of this, and deftly avoids handing negative news to the screening interviewer.

Screening interviews are generally not a good source of information for any specific details about the job. In fact, the more questions you raise with the screening interviewer, the more opportunities you have to bump into areas that are perceived as resistance. Rely on your research about the company and keep questions about the job at a high level. You will have ample opportunities to explore areas of compensation, benefits, travel, and other details after you pass the screening interview.

HOW SCREENING INTERVIEWS ARE EVALUATED AND REPORTED

Many seasoned recruiters and search professionals have a strong confidence in their ability to size up and quickly determine if a candidate is suitable to move on in the process. First and foremost, the screening interviewer's reputation is at stake. If there is anything that stands out as strange, quirky, or inconsistent about a candidate, it's far easier for the screening interviewer to move on to another candidate than to create a compelling reason to include the candidate in question.

In many cases, the final report will be based on the gut reaction of the interviewer. In other cases, particularly if the hiring company conducts it, the screening interview will be scored using preset criteria. While the scoring sheets may vary in detail, the general categories and outcomes are usually consistent. Screening interviews consistently evaluate a candidate on these criteria:

- **Job qualifications:** Do you have the experience, knowledge, and skills to do the job effectively? There may be specific criteria such as years in the field, degrees or technical training, size or scope of previous responsibilities, or industry-specific experience that is set with minimum criteria. Your responses should be affirmative and completely consistent with the information in your résumé.

- **Interest and motivation in the position:** What attracts you to the current position? Screening interviewers are most interested and need to be assured of the genuine commitment an interviewee has for a job. Make it easy for the screener to report back that you have done your research and have solid and insightful reasons for pursuing this particular job within this particular organization. Have two or three key examples of what specifically attracted you to the position.

- **Willingness to take on job-specific requirements:** Are you willing to take on the necessary aspects of the job, including travel and relocation? The screening interview is no place to begin negotiations on travel. If the job meets your criteria, the immediate response to job requirements should always be an unqualified yes.

- **Current situation and last position:** Why did you leave your last job and what are you doing now? This is a common question, one that can quickly become a source of turbulence in the screening interview if the response becomes complex and convoluted in any way. If your position was eliminated due to a reorganization or downsizing, state the facts. If you were terminated for any reason, a succinct explanation of a mutual decision should be provided with minimal details. If you are in transition, refer to self-improvement activities or consulting opportunities in addition to your search as your daily activities.
- **Salary qualifications:** In many screening interviews the question of salary will be raised to ensure that your salary history is commensurate with the position and that the offered salary range is of interest to you. If asked for your current salary, state your full salary, including any bonus structure and fringe benefits. If asked if a particular salary range is suitable for you, simply say yes, knowing that a no at this point could quickly end the interview process. You can always qualify your response with your need to understand more about the job before making a commitment. There will always be opportunities for salary negotiation when you get the offer.
- **Behavioral interview questions:** While the screening interview typically does not include time for a formal set of behavioral questions, some screeners slip one or two of these into the screening process. You should be prepared for a question or two of this type, as explained in the next chapter.

POWER STRATEGIES FOR SCREENING INTERVIEWS

If you understand that the purpose of screening interviews is to eliminate candidates, you can appreciate the fact that it is simply a hurdle you must clear to move forward on the race. Focus on that outcome

HireVue: The Future of Screening Interviews

It's often challenging for multiple contacts within a company to see the same candidate during screening interviews. The hiring manager and others in the organization typically want to review the candidates recruiters have passed on before bringing them on site. Enter HireVue.com, the leading provider of on-demand digital online, video-recorded interview technology. Their proprietary technology enables time shifting and place shifting. Companies engage candidates in initial interviews in a setting and time of the candidate's choice. All you need is a computer with a webcam or an iPhone, iPad, or iPod, and a high-speed Internet connection.

In a conversation with Chip Luman, COO of HireVue, Chip explained that candidates have three minutes to respond to the eight to ten questions asked in a typical interview. You have the opportunity to practice interview responses before your actual interview, and once the actual interview starts, your answers are recorded with no opportunity to correct your responses. Chip suggests that candidates prepare for the interview as they would for any other interview, know the company and position, make sure their attire and setting is professional, and check for good lighting and sound.

So lock the door, turn off your phone, keep the cat from jumping on your lap, and enjoy interviewing at home, in the library, or at the company you're hoping to work for. For more information, check out HireVue.com.

and you will be successful. Following are tips that will help you successfully navigate a screening interview:

- **Maintain your energy.** People who conduct screening interviews by phone typically contact many candidates and are easily fatigued or bored. A great way to maintain your energy is to stand up and move while you are on the phone. One of the best ways to keep your tone engaging is to smile. Try it!
- **Be concise.** Remember that people scoring screening interviews

typically have some sort of checklist or scoring form in front of them. Provide clear and concise answers that allow them to check the box quickly.

• **Be clear about nonnegotiables.** If you have set parameters around travel, relocation, or span of accountabilities that are truly nonnegotiable, be clear and direct. It would be better to end the process quickly than to be drawn into a selection process that will not take you to victory.

• **Be honest about your salary history.** If asked for your current salary, state it clearly, including bonus structure, merit, options, and perks. Companies can easily verify salary history.

• **Avoid negotiation.** Remember that the individual conducting the screening interview is likely to have little input on the final hiring decision, including salary. If asked if a salary range is acceptable, simply say yes or differ by saying you want to understand more about the opportunity. A no will most likely end the conversation.

ASKING QUESTIONS DURING THE SCREENING INTERVIEW

Screening interviews typically end with the interviewer asking the question, "Do you have any questions for me?" At this point, it's useful to have one or two very specific questions prepared that will reinforce your overall interest and commitment to pursuing the job opportunity.

You might mention a part of the job listing that is of particular interest or is well aligned with your capabilities. You might also ask the interviewer about their perspective or experience with the organization. In any case, it's important not to put the screening interviewer on the stand to defend any aspect of the organization or the job in question. Any probing questions and reservations about the position can be thoroughly explored when you are passed on to the main interview process.

The final and most important question to ask in the screening interview is, "What are the next steps in the process?" You will most likely be told that the information collected will be reviewed by the hiring manager or the selection committee, and you will be contacted. Politely ask, "In what time frame can I expect a response?" Having a clear idea of timing gives you a sense of how quickly the organization is moving and gives you a solid basis for following up with the organization if you have not heard from them in the time stated.

Screening interviews are standard operating procedures for most companies and recruiting agencies. If you anticipate the key "weed out" questions and deftly respond in a way that doesn't get you immediately eliminated, you always have the possibility to explore the opportunity in greater detail in the next conversation. Chances are, the individual you are talking to is not in a position to answer detailed questions about the job and company.

Remember that the screening interview is also your opportunity to make fast and informed decisions about the potential fit and suitability of the opportunity and the organization. If you encounter a knockout factor from your perspective, you'll save yourself a great deal of time and energy by making your own decision to end the interview process at this stage. Simply do so politely and directly at the end of the screening interview.

CHAPTER TEN
Hurdle Five: The Main Interview Process

———————◆————————————————◆———————

Once you have been passed through the screening interviews, the race will most likely continue to a series of interviews with individuals directly involved in the hiring decision. The interview process remains one of the most powerful and deciding influences in the race for selection.

Individuals who interview well can overcome significant barriers to being hired and compete successfully with candidates who have far more experience and skills. By understanding and responding directly to the needs of the organization and positioning themselves effectively, they can quickly move from an also ran to a front-runner.

WHY INTERVIEWS STILL WIN THE DAY

With all the technology and science associated with a modern selection process, you'd think that the interview would be just another factor in a long list of objective data that goes into the hiring decision. While other data points do impact hiring decisions, the outcome of the interview stands alone in its power to shape those decisions. There are at least three good reasons why the interview is so influential; studying these reasons will help you prepare to deliver your most powerful performance:

1. **First impressions are indelible.** Business people are consistently rewarded for their ability to size up people quickly and tend to do this within the first few minutes of interaction. People take cues from dress, stature, demeanor, facial expression, tone of voice, and eye contact to make immediate inferences about the individual. This initial impression will color the perception of you as a candidate for the foreseeable future.

2. **The decision to hire someone is a buying decision.** All buying decisions have an emotional component. The interview sets the tone for the emotional relationship between the candidate and the interviewer. The greater and the more positive the emotional component of your interaction, the more valuable you are perceived to be.

3. **Fit becomes obvious.** The question of fit within the culture of the hiring organization is most clearly answered in the interview process. Interviewers sum up many different qualities and attributes of the candidate during the interview and project these attributes onto a person they see successfully filling the role. Any significant departure from fit discovered in the interview will come up for discussion in the hiring decision.

Given the power of interviews to impact hiring decisions, preparation for the setup and clearing of this hurdle is among the most important in the race.

PREPARING FOR YOUR INTERVIEWS: VISUALIZING THE PROCESS

Successful hurdlers prepare by visualizing the hurdles and imagine themselves approaching, lifting, clearing, and landing each jump smoothly and swiftly. Before you dig into the details and specifics of interview structure, format, and preparation, it's good to develop a general approach and visualization of how you will begin, deliver, and conclude all of your interview experiences. Just as the athlete breaks down his or her approach and execution, you can train by breaking down each successful interview into three key components.

The Approach: Initial Interaction and Connections

Think about your style and approach to every new business introduction. How do you make the interaction relaxed, inviting, and affirmative? What cues or mannerisms do you look for in the individual you're meeting for the first time? What questions do you ask to break the ice?

The first minute of every interview process sets the stage and the trajectory for all the interaction that follows. The successful interviewee knows that the firm handshake, direct eye contact, and a sincere smile will open the door. From there, the experienced interviewer will typically direct you where to sit and open with some sort of small talk. This can be the golden moment of the interview. People have an inherent desire to make connections; any piece of common ground in history, industry experience, education, or career path can help forge the beginning of a relationship that will shape the balance of the interview.

The Jump: Discovering and Meeting Needs

The primary goal of a successful interview is not for you to dazzle the interviewer. Your core mission is to uncover the true needs for the position *from the perspective of the interviewer* and then skillfully cast your experience and abilities as an ideal fit for those needs. "Dazzling" focuses on promoting yourself. "Meeting needs" focuses on you being perceived as the ideal candidate. You will be a more successful candidate if you set your sites on the latter.

You have two significant opportunities during the interview to shape your profile to the needs of the job: answering questions and asking questions. Both skills are essential for the successful interview. A highly competitive interviewee is well practiced in, and prepared for, both sharing and seeking information. The more quality information shared in both directions, the stronger the set of connections that differentiate the strongest competitor.

The Landing: Conclusions and Next Steps

Strong interviews end on a solid note. The experienced interviewee reads the composure and body language of the interviewer and is acutely aware of the time allotted for the interview (without looking at his or her watch). Interviews typically end with the opportunity for the interviewee to ask questions. This is a great time to explore key areas of the position for which you will discover and meet needs.

A great way to wrap up your side of the interview is to summarize key points of connection between your understanding of key needs in the position and your ability to meet those needs. Hand back the direction of the interview by simply asking, "Is there any additional information you need from me?" This will allow the interviewer to end the interview and direct you to any next steps, including the next appointment on the interview schedule.

A strong visualization and expectation of (1) how the interview will flow and (2) the core objectives you wish to achieve will help you maintain the presence, focus, and energy necessary to fully engage the interviewer.

LISTENING: THE MOST POWERFUL SKILL IN INTERVIEWING

As many job candidates prepare for the hurdle of interviews, they become completely focused on themselves. They focus on their story, their jobs, their accomplishments, their strengths, and their delivery. While solid technique and powerful delivery are essential for successful interviewing, a singular focus on self can also be a detriment to the most important aspect and fundamental skill of interviewing: hearing and responding to the needs of the organization.

Companies do not hire top leadership positions lightly. When considering a million-dollar-plus investment in an individual, a company has well-established, identified needs in filling the role. If the organization did not have a strong and particular need, it would be far easier to allow the revenues needed to fill the position to fall to the bottom line. The first priority of the successful interviewee is to understand for what purposes the organization is willing to make this investment.

From the beginning of the networking and sourcing process, seek information to help you understand precisely what the organization is looking for in this particular position. In addition to your research on the organization, great sources of information include the job listing and any inside information that can be provided by your recruiting contacts.

It's essential to understand why the position is currently open. Was there an incumbent who was removed from the organization and, if so, for what reason? Is this a new position that is been added to the organizational structure and, if so, what is driving that investment? Understanding the fundamental rationale and objectives of the organization in making a hire is job one in preparing for the interview process.

DETERMINING WHY YOUR INTERVIEWERS WERE SELECTED

The individuals chosen for the interview process says much about the culture of the organization. Flattened organizational structures drive consensus decisions. You might interview with a broad array of potential peers and subordinates in addition to business area leaders. You may even have group interviews with large groups of constituencies. In a more traditional, hierarchical organization, you may interview with just a few, select leaders or committee members directly related to your position. Understanding why your interviewers were selected will help you understand organizational drivers and needs.

As you prepare for interviews, answer at least three questions for each individual with whom you will interview:

1. Why has this person been selected for the interview process? What are his or her top two or three business needs to be met by this hire?
2. If hired, how will your new role interface with this individual? How can you ensure that your skills, experience, and objectives will be aligned with his or her position?
3. What do you know about the background and history of the interviewer? A careful review of a biography or LinkedIn profile is critical prep work for each individual with whom you are interviewing.

By answering these questions, you prepare yourself to be an open and receptive listener, positioned to respond fully to the needs and interests of each person with whom you are interviewing.

Winning the Race by Meeting the Real Need

Marianne never thought she had a chance at the job of senior director of Information Systems at Dargon, Inc. In her fifteen years of IT experience, she had implemented and upgraded several proprietary ERP systems, but she had little familiarity with the SAP solution that Dargon had been working on for the last three years. The position posting clearly stated that five years of SAP experience was required.

Marianne got an opportunity to talk with Jonathan, the VP of Global IT at Dargon, through a network connection. This was initially a courtesy call based on a long-term relationship with a mutual colleague. After initial introductions, Marianne just allowed Jonathan to talk. He lamented about the many things that had gone awry in the SAP implementation process: poor end-user adoption, misalignment with business unit priorities, general resistance to standardization, and a significant downturn in system funding during the recession.

Marianne listened. And heard a deep need.

Jonathan had never had the end-user training support he felt he needed. In response, Marianne told him the story of how, faced with a similar situation, she sourced an innovative training vendor who provided a cutting-edge blended learning solution, which greatly enhanced the speed and effectiveness of her implementation. Jonathan heard something that he valued far more than five years of SAP experience. He understood that Marianne could think, understand complex issues, and drive for a unique solution. Marianne was on her way to becoming a finalist for a position she thought was out of her reach.

INTERVIEWING WITH POTENTIAL PEERS AND SUBORDINATES

Many organizations are waking up to the value of having peers and subordinates interview candidates for leadership positions. Giving these employees an active voice in the hiring decision greatly supports their buy-in for the decision. When interviewing with people who may be your peers or direct reports in the near future, keep in mind that there are at least two critical questions they will ask themselves during the interview:

1. Is this a person I could see myself working with or working for on a day-to-day basis?
2. Does this person represent a potential threat to my job or career stability?

These questions will not likely be discussed openly in candidate review meetings, but the conclusions that interviewers draw will strongly influence their level of support for you. It's not uncommon for candidacy to be undone by the political maneuvering of people who see you as a threat or challenge.

With this in mind, it's essential when interviewing with potential peers and subordinates to instill confidence as a leader, not to overwhelm or intimidate them with your accomplishments or deep industry knowledge. Your best strategy for achieving this outcome is to strike a balance between you learning about them and them learning about you. Take an active and sincere interest in their perspective, accomplishments, and future aspirations; this will demonstrate your commitment and support for them as colleagues.

UNDERSTANDING INTERVIEW FORMATS

As you approach interview preparation it's helpful to understand that the interview hurdle can be separated into general interview types. Knowing the structure, intent, and delivery of each type of interview will help you to clear these hurdles with the power, timing, and grace essential to victory.

THE BEHAVIORAL INTERVIEW

There's been much research and scientific study imposed on the interview process. In some organizations, a standardized approach has permeated the entire process and is commonly known as the behavioral interview. All competitive candidates know the structure, outcomes, and superior response technique to the behavioral interview format.

Behavioral interviewing is based on scientific principles. Properly conducted, the process is a precise and effective means of differentiating candidates' past experience and potential for future performance. People responsible for designing and evaluating behavioral interviews (typically industrial organizational psychologists or similarly trained human resource professionals) will ensure that interviews are conducted and evaluated consistently with a standard operating procedure. Continuity and consistency in the interviewing process assures that candidates are measured against a valid and reliable measuring stick and that comparisons between candidates are meaningful.

Behavioral interviewing is based on a three-part process:

1. Determining key competencies that will differentiate success in the position.
2. Asking the candidate to provide specific examples where they have demonstrated these competencies in the past.
3. Assessing the candidate's response based on a generally objective set of criteria.

Accordingly, preparation for the behavioral interview requires you to prepare in three steps.

Step One: Anticipate Which Competencies Will Be Assessed

While all organizations using behavioral interviews have their own set of competencies that are defined at each level of management, the list for leadership competencies tends to be fairly consistent. The appendix of this book provides a good overview of some of the competencies most often used for mid- to senior-level management selection. Some leadership competencies most frequently assessed at the senior level include strategic insight, command skills, integrity, customer focus, people development, team leadership, and organizational insight.

The organization may also include interview questions about technical and functional competencies. These are harder to anticipate in that technical competencies will be related to the specific demands of the position. The best way to anticipate technical and functional interview questions is to carefully and precisely review the job listing. In some cases, the leadership and technical competencies are actually listed in the position description. Any additional information you can gain from your search professional or networking activities will help you zero in on key competencies that will be assessed for the position.

Step Two: Prepare Behavioral-Based Responses

Most behavioral interview questions begin with a similar prompt, such as "Tell me about a time when . . ." or "Could you give me an example where you have accomplished _____ in a past position?" In all cases, the question asks you to recount a specific situation in which you demonstrated the competency in question.

Your initial response should be a one- to two-minute summary that follows the CAR formula that you used to develop your platform:

- **Challenge:** Briefly describe the situation in which you specifically addressed the opportunity to take action. Explain how you thought about the opportunity and what led you to take the course of action you took.
- **Action:** Describe the specific actions that you took to address

Blowing Away the Wrong Person

Eduardo could hardly wait for his interview with Rachel, the vice president of Marketing. In Eduardo's previous experience as a product manager and design engineer, he had worked closely with his marketing department, directing entire product launch campaigns from start to finish. He had carefully crafted his experiences into a compelling series of case studies. In each story he had successfully led the marketing professionals to implement his thoughtfully articulated, step-by-step approaches.

As the interview started, Eduardo launched into his repertoire of successful product launches and how he had carefully educated his marketing department on the needs of the customer, pointing out compelling design features, and even selecting the preferred media channels and graphics vendors. All Eduardo could think about was how impressed Rachel would be with his ability to be a knowledgeable partner.

As Rachel listened to the pitch and nodded her head intently, all she could think about was how difficult it would be to contain and redirect a person who knows it all and has a preconceived idea of how to run her department. In the interview debrief, it was easy for Rachel to jump on board with a general theme that Eduardo would not be a team player, quickly ending his candidacy.

the issue or opportunity in broad strokes. Avoid getting into any unnecessary detail. It's fine to mention the supporting actions of others but the example should focus on actions that you directed or delegated.

- **Results:** Summarize the key results of the actions that you took in the situation. Frame the results in specific metrics whenever possible, including measurable changes that resulted directly from your actions.

Anticipate that the interviewer will have a few follow-up prompts to elicit more information on your experience. Listen carefully to the prompts, as they are often used to dig deeper, verify information, or fill in a gap in the initial response. If you see that the interviewer is satisfied with the response, allow the interview to move on to the next question. If you feel the interviewer is looking for additional information, you can ask, "Have I fully answered your question?" Use this technique sparingly, as asking it too often may signal that you are unsure of your responses.

There's only one good way to get good at behavioral event interviewing: prepare and practice. A strong candidate will have developed a core set of ten to twelve CAR responses that can be shaped to focus on the key competencies for the position. There's no better way to prepare for the behavioral event interview than to enlist a friend to ask you behavioral questions. Record your responses on a voice or video recording. As you listen to the playback of your responses, make notes of opportunities for improvement. The last place you want to start practicing your behavioral event interviewing skills is in the middle of a high-stakes interview process.

Step Three: Anticipate the Interview Scoring Process

It's difficult to win a race if you don't know the rules by which the winner is chosen. Unfortunately, there are no precise and standard rules governing how a behavioral-based interview will be assessed or how interview data will be used to compare candidates. There are common and consistent approaches for evaluating interviews, and in more formal and structured organizations these criteria and processes are used more consistently. As a strong interviewee, you will consider how the interview will be evaluated and comparisons made after you leave.

Typically, a debrief session is scheduled at the end of each interview process. All the interviewers attend this debriefing, which is sometimes coordinated by a recruiter or HR staff member. The agenda typically includes a summary by each individual of what they saw as the strengths or weaknesses of each candidate, with clear examples from their interviews to support their conclusions. In many cases, interviewers are asked to rate candidates on each assessed competency on a one-to-five scale, with five being "outstanding."

Recognizing and Responding to Learning Agility Questions

The concept of learning agility is quickly finding its way into the behavioral interviewing process. As we reviewed in chapter 5, learning agility is the capacity to actively learn from past experiences and apply these insights in new situations. As research and writing on the concept of learning agility spreads as a key indicator of potential to succeed in new roles, learning agility prompts are being integrated into standard interview protocols.

Interviewers who are trained to look for learning agility will typically include at least two follow-up prompts for each behavioral interview question: 1) What did you learn from this experience? and 2) How did you apply what you learned in a future situation?

Well-prepared candidates will quickly recognize the concepts of learning agility and will respond with an appropriate example of how they learned a core principle or strategy from one situation and actively applied it in another. Even if the learning agility prompts are not integrated into your interview, using examples of how you used learning from experience to guide your actions in future situations is a powerful way to differentiate your performance in an interview.

POWER STRATEGIES TO ENSURE HIGH BEHAVIORAL INTERVIEW SCORES

Following are specific strategies to make sure that you are scored and presented as positively as possible in the interview debrief session:

- Think about the specific leadership competency implied by the question. Use that key word or words to shape your response.
- Make it easy for the interviewer to score you positively on each behavioral-based question with a full response based on the CAR formula.
- Always present your results in clear and tangible terms using data, dollar figures, percentages, and other appropriate metrics. Drawing from specific examples in your résumé will reinforce key messages.

- In your response, take full accountability for the initiation and outcomes of all actions taken. It's great to talk about a team effort but define your unique contribution to the outcome. Avoid blaming circumstances or failure of others for an outcome.
- Stay focused on the precise question asked by the interviewer. Meandering off topic or providing ancillary examples that don't relate to the question will steer you away from the top score.

There is only one sure way to ensure you do as well as possible in a debrief session. Practice delivering complete, concise, and compelling responses (with feedback) well in advance of an actual interview.

SCENARIO-BASED QUESTIONS

Another variation on the behavioral event interview question is a scenario-based question. In this variation, you are given the brief description of a hypothetical situation, then asked how you would respond to the challenge it presents. The scenario-based interview adds an interesting twist to the process. In some cases there is a "right" or at least a best type of response and your performance will be scored to that reference point.

Scenario-based questions are often related to key competencies and typically focus on judgment, decision making, and problem solving. Interviewers also like to add a human element to scenarios as well. Typical scenario-based questions include difficult situations in which any course of action yields a potential negative outcome:

- An initiative that is supported by top management is stiffly resisted by middle management.
- An employee shows great leadership potential but is unwilling to accept feedback on a critical flaw.
- A customer demands a significant discount on a product due to

late shipment and threatens to cancel the order if the discount is not awarded.

Solid answers to the situations require a balanced view, capacity for solid communications, and decisive action.

POWER STRATEGIES FOR SCENARIO-BASED QUESTIONS

Scenario-based questions are more difficult to anticipate than behavioral questions, but there are several key strategies you can implement to ensure your highest performance:

- Your research on the company and knowledge of the position supplies the context to answer the question fully and succinctly. Some scenarios may be driven by actual events in the organization, so linking your specific knowledge based on your research can add power to your response.
- Listen to the scenario carefully. There are often important clues embedded in scenario-based questions that point to specific information that will shape a successful response.
- As you think about the question, a good starting point to collect your thoughts is to determine (a) what additional information you would need to respond to the situation, and (b) where and how you would collect that information. "It depends . . ." may be an appropriate way to start your response, but don't use lack of data as an excuse to avoid answering the question.
- You can ask the interviewer for additional information about the situation, but don't overuse this approach as it may seem like you're fishing for the right answer.
- Use the CAR formula for your response, with specific emphasis on thinking through the challenge and the desired outcome.

Your results will be hypothetical and should be shaped to be definitive and measurable.

For example, if you were interviewing for an operations position, you might be told that one of your facilities had a sudden drop in profitability although your sales and gross revenues are strong. This is a broad-based scenario and the interviewer is looking for your experience and critical thinking related to factors impacting profitability. An appropriate answer would demonstrate a thorough knowledge of all the principal factors impacting the plant's ability to ship and invoice consistently and may touch on quality, productivity, or supply issues.

A solid answer would be to describe clearly what data would be assessed, what potential problems would be identified, and what clear actions would be taken to overcome those issues. A strong response to a scenario-based question ends with a summary of the results that would be achieved if these actions were taken.

AD HOC INTERVIEW QUESTIONS

Many companies have not implemented structured, behavioral interview formats, or if they have, it's not uncommon for senior to executive managers to dismiss the process. Having had some success with a set of standard questions, many hiring managers and senior executives tend to ask the same questions over and over again, regardless of how they may be directed by HR staff or talent management professionals.

While it is impossible to anticipate every ad hoc interview question, there are some general types of questions that are commonly asked in some variation. Listed next is a hit list of twenty common interview questions that provide a strong base on which to practice and prepare for the ad hoc interview question:

1. Tell me about yourself.
2. What interests you about this position and our organization?

3. What professional accomplishments are you most proud of?

4. What are your greatest strengths?

5. Tell me about your weaknesses.

6. How would you describe your leadership style?

7. What strategies do you use to see that your goals are accomplished?

8. What leaders have had the greatest influence in your life? What did you learn from them?

9. What are your professional goals?

10. How do you define success at work? At this point do you consider yourself successful?

11. Tell me about a successful project or initiative that you have led. What was the impact of your actions on the business?

12. Why did you leave your past position?

13. Describe your relationship with your former boss. What did you learn from this relationship?

14. How do you manage conflict in the workplace?

15. Describe a situation in which you dealt with failure.

16. What have you been doing while you are not employed (or explain a gap in your employment history)?

17. In what areas do you need to develop to be successful in this position?

18. What are your plans to continue your education and professional development?

19. What is a unique value that you can add to our organization?

20. Why should we hire you over other candidates?

The best way to prepare for ad hoc interview questions is to develop core strategies that you will use in response to all questions. Listed here are five general strategies for answering interview questions in a way that conveys your true strengths:

1. **Be concise**. Address the question directly and specifically. One of the most common and detrimental interviewing

blunders is to talk around the question or provide too much detail. Initial responses should be forty-five seconds to three minutes maximum.

2. **Be modest.** Describe your thinking and actions in a clear and matter-of-fact tone and describe your accomplishments as natural outcomes of your actions. Avoid boasting or bragging about your successes. Arrogance can be the kiss of death in any interview process.

3. **Be positive.** Always describe situations and people leading toward a positive outcome. Never, ever, speak disparagingly or in a negative way about former bosses, peers, or organizations.

4. **Be authentic.** Don't be afraid to share your true thoughts or feelings about a situation. Being candid and open can deepen the sense of trust and relationship with the interviewer. Very brief, personal anecdotes that communicate your fear or frustration can add depth to your message. Just stay away from statements that would cast you in a negative light.

5. **End on a high note.** Interviewers tend to be most impacted by the first and last part of the response. Make a habit of concluding your responses with a positive outcome, lesson learned, or expectation for the future.

There are many sources of typical interview questions available online and in books specifically dedicated to the interviewing process. It's not possible to anticipate and be prepared for every ad hoc question, but having a solid sense of techniques and principles learned in your interview preparation will ready you for any question directed your way.

ASKING QUESTIONS: THE LEVERAGE POINT FOR BUILDING CONNECTIONS

As the interview process progresses, there will inevitably be a time for you to ask questions. The questions that you ask will have as much

The Age-old Question of Discussing Your Weaknesses

One of the most anticipated questions in the interview process is the discussion of your shortcomings. Every hiring decision will end up in some form of discussion of pros and cons about the candidate. At some point in the interview process, every interviewer will ask about your cons.

Actively shape the perception of your shortcomings as challenges that you have successfully addressed:

1. Discuss your shortcoming as an occasionally overused strength. For example, you might cite your strong bias for action includes the opportunity to slow down, to take others ideas and data into consideration.

2. Discuss a developmental opportunity that you have successfully managed in the past. For example, you might explain that while finance was not part of your formal education, you took additional courses or self-study to remedy this deficit.

3. Discuss how you have effectively engaged resources or support that complement an area that is not a natural strength for you. For example, you might discuss how your last hire had the strengths of structure and process that complemented your creative style.

The idea here is not to deny that you have limitations, but to show your awareness of your areas of challenge and your active responses to those challenges.

bearing on your success as the questions you answer. Careful thought and preparation is necessary to frame engaging and meaningful questions that will clearly differentiate your interest and commitment from that of other candidates.

Find the optimal balance in asking questions during the interview. On one hand, you want to ask sincere, insightful questions that clearly indicate that they need to sell you on this opportunity. On the other hand, you don't want to come across as arrogant or dismissive of the opportunity by putting your interviewer on trial. The secret to striking this balance is to focus on your primary goal: to cast yourself as the ideal candidate who understands and responds to the needs of the organization.

POWER STRATEGIES FOR ASKING QUESTIONS

The goal of your questions in your first interview is to discover the needs of the organization specifically related to the role. Questions should start with immediate needs for the position, and then build to future needs and the broader organizational strategy:

- **Understand the immediate goals for this position.** Focus your initial questions on understanding the primary objectives of the job from the interviewer's perspective. Find out the history of the position and what the interviewer defines as top performance outcomes looking forward. Ask about the incumbent, but avoid dwelling on any personal failures or shortcomings.
- **Understand the future of the job.** Ask the interviewer where he or she sees a successful hire taking the role in the next two to three years. What specific challenges must be addressed? What key capabilities will be needed to meet these challenges? What are the career possibilities beyond this role?
- **Define core, strategic objectives for the company.** This may include general growth strategy, capital investment, new product or service offerings, acquisition activities, and competitive challenges. You should have at least two to three relevant and specific questions prepared based on your research of the company. Relate this back to the purpose and outcome of your target position.
- **Explore the fit.** Ask about the general culture of the organization in areas of interest to you (e.g., hierarchy, decision making, autonomy, functional interactions, and interaction style with the CEO and board). Focusing on the interviewer's perspective of the company is a great transition into wrap-up.

- **Watch closely for time and pacing.** Wrap up your questioning by making two or three major connections that directly align with your interests, career trajectory, and past experience.

If you can accomplish these outcomes in the typical hour slotted for the initial interview, you have accomplished much. The interviewer will see both your fit and your enthusiasm for the position.

There are also a few areas to actively avoid in an initial interview. This is not the time to discuss any issues or barriers to your taking the job. Any reservations you have about travel, relocation, commute, salary, or part of the job that does not fit your expectations can be discussed in subsequent meetings (and preferably after you have an offer).

POWER OR "STRESS" INTERVIEWS

Although not nearly as prevalent as they once were, some organizations will purposely insert stress or distractions into the interview process to see how you handle difficult or ambiguous situations. Typical strategies for stress interviewing includ:

- Having individuals interrupt or derail an interview
- Asking provocative, challenging, "in your face" kind of questions
- Actively arguing or criticizing your responses

These types of interviews have gotten a bad rap because they can give a very negative initial impression of the organization and often result in the candidate questioning whether he or she wants to work for the organization. At the same time, challenging senior leadership positions require people who can handle stress, ambiguity, and demonstrate poise in intense meeting situations. Regardless of how you feel about contrived interview situations, your best bet is to be prepared.

In some cases, a stress interview may not be planned by the organization, but a specific interviewer may believe that this is an effective approach. This is often the case in a sales-related position where the interviewer wants to see if you can actually handle a difficult customer. In this situation you have been given a great opportunity to be polite, professional, and never back down. You have a far better chance of doing well in the interview if you stand up to anything that is thrown at you.

POWER STRATEGIES FOR RESPONDING TO STRESS INTERVIEWS

Remember that any interview will have its stressful moments, planned or unplanned; these strategies may come in handy in any stress-provoking situation:

- **Anticipate the approach.** Do your homework on the organization and company profiles, particularly on reader reviews on social networking or company profiling websites. Many times an organization has a reputation for using stress interview tactics.
- **Do not to avoid the challenge.** Anticipate the unfavorable reactions that interviewers will interpret as weaknesses or lack of preparation: silence, freezing, retreat, or excuses. Make an active decision that you are not going to respond with these behaviors.
- **Use verbal jujitsu.** The art of jujitsu is to take the energy of the attacker and redirect it. One of the best ways to respond to an attack is to acknowledge the attackers point of view and ask them to clarify their assumptions and thinking. Pulling them into a conversation rather than refuting them gives you a chance to redirect their attack.
- **Practice basic negotiation skills.** One of the basic skills of negotiation is to understand the principle or premise on which you and an adversary can agree. If you can get a detractor to

agree to something reasonable, you're moving the conversation forward. If not, you're exposing the individual as argumentative.

- **Take control of the meeting.** The key question on the outcome of a stress interview is, "Did the candidate maintain control of the situation?" There's no better way to do this than to actively clarify the agenda of the meeting and to respectfully and consistently request that individuals return to that agenda.

You have undoubtedly responded to heated, confrontational, or disruptive situations in your career. You can certainly rely on that experience and confidence if you should encounter a tense situation in an interview whether or not it is contrived.

ESTABLISHING NEXT STEPS

One of the most challenging and potentially frustrating aspects of the selection race is waiting to hear back from organizations about reactions to the interview and the timeline for a hiring decision. There are many factors that may delay an organization's response to a candidate. Some of the most common reasons for delay include scheduling of additional candidates, finding times for selection committee members to meet, getting final budget approval, and waiting for the results of background checks to be completed. Unfortunately, organizations are sometimes less than timely and consistent in getting back to candidates.

The best way to manage this situation is to ask the hiring manager or the individual coordinating the interview process to identify the next step and the approximate timeline when a response can be expected. Leaving the interview process without this established opens you up to all sorts of mental gymnastics and unnecessary worry as you wait for the phone to ring. Internal recruiting professionals and hiring managers are sensitive to this issue and are fully prepared to give you a response.

FOLLOWING UP WITH INTERVIEWERS

It's customary to follow up with a brief note to interviewers within twenty-four hours of the interview. A brief e-mail sent during regular business hours on the first business day following the interview demonstrates appropriate timing and business etiquette. Written notes sent by regular mail add a personal touch but may take too long for the interviewer to receive. Ideally, a follow-up note will express your appreciation for the interviewers' time and consideration and, very briefly, summarize any key connections made in the interview process. In many cases you may receive a response from an interviewer, which is always a positive sign in building relationships.

Despite all the changes and innovations in the world of candidate selection, there is no more important or decisive event in your race than the face-to-face interview. HR and recruiting professionals will weigh in on the process with objective data, assessments, reports on references, and background checks. All of these points will be considered in the decision, but the final choice will be most influenced by the connections made with the people who will choose to work with you.

The key to great interviewing is simple. Focus on filling the needs of the organization, be genuine, understand the agenda of individuals with whom you are interviewing, and listen carefully. This is simple, but it's not necessarily easy. Great interviewing takes practice. You can choose to practice on the first several job opportunities you encounter or you can choose to work with an experienced colleague or professional. In either case, your interviewing skills will only increase with time, experience, and accurate feedback.

CHAPTER ELEVEN

Hurdle Six: Psychological and Cognitive Assessments

The job candidate competing in today's market can fully expect to encounter some aspect of standardized assessment as an important hurdle in the race for selection. The more you understand the purpose, structure, and outcomes of standardized assessments, the more prepared you will be to give your best performance.

STANDARDIZED ASSESSMENTS AND THE LAW

The use of standardized assessments and hiring practices in general are governed by several acts of Congress, including the Civil Rights Act, the Age Discrimination in Employment Act, and the Equal Employment Opportunity Commission. In addition, proper use of assessments is directed by the guidelines of the American Psychological Association and other professional associations.

Based on professional and government scrutiny and with the potential for litigation related to unfair hiring practices, organizations using standardized assessments should support these fair use criteria:

- The assessment process is unbiased and fair to all groups including age, race, ethnic group, and gender.
- The standardized assessment measures traits or criteria that are directly related to performance on the job (the assessment is valid).
- The standardized assessment is used consistently for all job candidates for a given position.

There have been several cases of civil litigation directed at the use of standardized assessments over the years. As a result, vendors and organizations that use these tools have become more vigilant about fair and standard use, particularly at the mid-management and executive levels. If you are requested to take standardized assessments with a reputable organization, the process has most likely received a reasonable level of scrutiny.

You certainly have the right to refuse to take an assessment, but it's likely that you would then not be considered for the position. If you have a documented disability that would impact your performance on an assessment, you can legally request that limitation be accommodated in the assessment process.

HOW ASSESSMENT SCORES INFLUENCE SELECTION DECISIONS

If you ask any human resource professional or hiring manager how they use standardized assessment scores in their hiring process, the most immediate response is likely to be, "Assessment scores are just part of the equation; we consider the candidate as a whole person."

This is a standard and well-intentioned response. In practice, however, assessment scores tend to have disproportionately strong bearing on hiring decisions, particularly if the assessment data are negative in any way. Here are some of the reasons why assessments are so influential:

- Unlike résumé, references, and interview ratings, assessment data is seen as objective and unbiased.
- If there are several qualified candidates for a position, it is an easy choice to tag strong scores as a key differentiator in decision making.
- Selecting a candidate who did not do well on an assessment can be seen as a significant risk. A common question when a new hire does not work out is, "How did that person do in their pre-employment assessments?"

There are several types of assessments commonly used in mid- to high-level management positions. As a competitor, it is crucial that you understand what each type of assessment measures, how it is related to expectations for the position, and how you can best prepare for taking the assessment.

PERSONALITY ASSESSMENTS

Personality assessments are one of the most common forms of pre-employment testing. They have been shown to be accurate (strong predictive validity) in identifying strengths and potential limitations of candidates. Modern personality assessments are derived from decades of academic research on the nature and structure of the personality. Most personality assessments trace their origin to a few core personality theories and are based on similar assumptions. The first is that some traits of the personality are relatively stable over time and these can be measured accurately through self-reported assessments. The second assumption is that these traits are related to future job performance.

Personality assessments used for candidate screening vary a great deal in structure and format, but some of the key traits that they measure are relatively consistent. A good start for understanding what personality assessments can measure is to consider the traits underlying the Big Five Theory of personality, a theoretical foundation for many common personality assessments.

Listed below is a brief description of each of the Big Five traits:

1. **Extraversion:** This trait is related to openness and may be indicated by preferences for talkativeness, social interaction, and assertiveness.
2. **Agreeableness:** People who score high on this trait demonstrate positive social interactions, including kindness, affection, appreciation, and mutual support.
3. **Conscientiousness:** This trait includes the tendency to be organized, a planner, detail-oriented, and thorough.
4. **Neuroticism:** Individuals with this trait tend to experience anxiety, moodiness, and sadness. This trait may indicate emotional instability.
5. **Openness:** People with this trait tend to have a wide range of interests and tend to be imaginative and insightful.

It's easy to see how these traits may indicate a better fit for certain types of jobs. For example, extraversion would support roles where initiating contacts and promoting ideas are essential, such as sales or senior leadership. Conscientiousness would be a desirable trait for roles that require precision and follow through, such as engineering or accounting. Openness is key trait for people who are accountable for developing new ideas and leading the organization in new directions. Agreeableness would be important in roles and in organizations that emphasize teamwork and collaboration. Tendencies for anxiety or sadness may be indications of low tolerance for stress.

In general, personality tests are selected and configured for specific profiles and levels of management defined by the hiring organization. In many cases, the scores derived from a personality assessment are reported in comparison to the "perfect candidate" who reports the ideal configuration of traits. The hiring recommendation report typically includes a score on each of the composite attributes and an overall score indicating fit or likely success in the position. In some cases, an overall hiring recommendation is made by the report.

There are also personality-based assessments designed for specific job profiles. The most common of these are sales assessments that include profiles for direct sales and sales management. Common traits that are assessed by sales profiles include persistence, extraversion, stress resistance, willingness to overcome objections, and decisiveness. The best way to ensure your best performance of the sales assessment is to take the assessment in the same frame of mind and even the same time of day that you actively sell. Taking a sales assessment at home after two glasses of merlot will not have you centered in a selling frame of mind.

GAMING PERSONALITY ASSESSMENTS

One of the most common questions about personality assessments from both candidates and hiring organizations is if people can easily misrepresent themselves on personality tests. The clear and obvious answer is yes. Most personality assessments are based on the reporting of the candidate and the data collected online with some level of privacy. This gives candidates every opportunity to shape their answers in any way they want. As tempting as it may be to want to "play" the assessment and to get the best scores, there are at least three solid arguments on why this is a limiting strategy:

- Personality assessments are valuable tools for candidates as well as hiring organizations. Indications of gaps and lack of fit can help you, the candidate, avoid the worst outcome possible: pursuing a position that is not a good fit for you.

• Personality assessments are carefully designed to measure an individual's tendency to make themselves appear too positive. If "social desirability" scores seem overly inflated, they can render the results invalid.

• Many hiring organizations use their pre-hire assessments as development and onboarding tools. There would be little value in this process if the results did not accurately represent your true personality profile.

The best approach for demonstrating an accurate and favorable profile on personality assessment is to respond to the items quickly and intuitively and not to overanalyze each item with the idea of presenting a particular profile.

STRATEGIES FOR TAKING PERSONALITY ASSESSMENTS

If your goal is to represent yourself accurately and consistently in a personality assessment, there are several strategies you can implement to ensure that your results reflect your true personality profile:

• Understand the purpose and outcomes of the assessment you're taking. It's not unreasonable to ask your recruiting contact about the nature of the test, although you should not anticipate a detailed explanation. If you are sent a link to the assessment from an administration site, research the vendor, and understand what the key selling points of the assessment are for the organization.

• Always read the instructions for an assessment carefully and completely. One of the most frequent errors candidates can make is to reverse rating scales, which typically results in a negative report. Organizations will typically refuse to reassess a candidate, seeing a failure to read instructions as an indication of poor performance.

- Maintain a focus on representing yourself the way you are in a work situation as opposed to how you may be at home or with family or friends.
- Avoid taking personality assessments in a situation where you are emotionally distraught (e.g., overly stressed, angry, frustrated, or sad). Temporary emotional conditions can reflect negatively on your results.
- Take the assessment thoughtfully, but don't try to overanalyze particular items.
- Your most useful and accurate responses will come from your first impression.

Perhaps the best advice for taking personality assessments is to take them openly, authentically, and thoughtfully.

COGNITIVE ASSESSMENTS

Cognitive assessments refer to any standardized assessments that measure the ability to analyze information and draw conclusions from that information—quickly and accurately. There are several types of cognitive assessments that are typically used in pre-employment testing. These include the following:

- **General intelligence:** These are general assessments that may include verbal, mathematical, or brief problem-solving items. The scores of these assessments are typically related to IQ or a general measure of intelligence.
- **Critical thinking:** These assessments are most often composed of descriptions of complex situations, such as excerpts from news articles. You are required to select the most reasonable conclusion or inference based on the information provided.
- **Verbal reasoning:** This type of an assessment may include

choosing the correct definition of vocabulary words or to complete word analogies.

- **Pattern Recognition:** These assessments may include a series of numbers, pictures, or abstract patterns and require that you fill in or select the next logical response to complete a sequence.

Unlike personality assessments, speed of completion is a critical factor in measurement, so cognitive assessments are typically timed.

Cognitive assessments have a long history of controversy and litigation related to bias toward specific groups. Despite these challenges, cognitive assessments have been consistently upheld by courts as fair and valid measures on which to base employment decisions. There is also substantial evidence correlating performance on cognitive assessments with objective measures of performance in the workplace. Cognitive assessments tend to have a solid impact in mid- to executive-level leadership positions. Given the choice, organizations will typically favor candidates who have been objectively identified with superior cognitive abilities.

CAN YOU IMPROVE YOUR PERFORMANCE ON COGNITIVE ASSESSMENTS?

General intelligence is a trait that is very stable and consistent over time. People who have been assessed at one level of intelligence do not typically change dramatically over time. There is little indication that any amount of studying of content or broad-based learning will help you do better on cognitive assessments in the short term. However, there is a growing body of evidence that you can increase your short- and long-term memory and speed of recall, which can improve performance on cognitive assessments.

Imagine that you show up for a hurdles race and hadn't jumped a hurdle since your attempt during track and field day in high school. You would be starting from scratch. Learning the process as you make your first attempt would be decidedly awkward and potentially painful. It would make a lot more sense for you to do some practice attempts before you enter your first race.

Consider taking timed, cognitive assessments to acclimate you to the feel and the flow of this kind of assessment before you take one that significantly affects your opportunity for the job. The Internet abounds with free IQ tests, games, and applications that can improve your short-term memory and problem-solving abilities and, most importantly, condition you to the feel of timed assessment. Something as simple as Sudoku or crossword puzzles can keep your brain active and focused.

POWER STRATEGIES FOR COGNITIVE ASSESSMENTS

In addition to actively engaging your mind in warm-up activities, the best way to improve your performance on cognitive assessments is by developing a solid set of test-taking strategies. These strategies will not make you smarter, but they will enable you to eliminate variables that could potentially detract from your score:

- Always take a cognitive assessment under the most favorable conditions for healthy thinking. Begin taking a cognitive assessment only when you are clearheaded, well rested, and in a positive mood. Never take an assessment when you are overly stressed, upset, or depressed.
- Be absolutely sure that you will not be interrupted during the assessment. The recruiting manager will not be impressed if you explain that the phone or the doorbell rang during your assessment and you didn't have time to complete it.
- Track and manage your time carefully throughout the assessment. Many assessments are progressively more difficult as you move through the exercise, so it's important not to rush through initial items that may be the easiest to complete correctly.

- Read the instructions for each section of the cognitive assessment carefully and take time to study any sample questions that illustrate how the items are constructed. This part of the assessment is typically not timed, so do not rush through instructions or sample questions.
- When taking critical thinking assessments, start by reading the question before you read the initial passage. This will help you identify key information as you read the initial passage. Skimming material too quickly can lead you to gloss over important words or concepts related to the correct answer.

In general, you will perform on cognitive assessments similarly to how you performed on standardized tests that you took throughout school, including aptitude tests and placement exams. If you scored consistently well and placed in the top percentages, your scores on cognitive assessments are typically not going to limit you in the selection process.

If you tend not to do well on standardized assessments, it would be a good idea to anticipate a moderate or low performance on your scores. In this case, you will have the chance to show evidence that you can and have successfully analyzed complex business situations and drawn accurate and timely conclusions and the test scores are an anomaly. Having clear and compelling examples of how you think and take action is by far the best way to counteract any negative indication based on a lower assessment score.

Most organizations are not keen on revealing the results of personality and cognitive assessment data to candidates unless they are hired, particularly if there were questionable results. It certainly cannot hurt to ask the organization for feedback as particular scores may come up for discussion directly or indirectly in subsequent interviews.

CHAPTER TWELVE
Hurdle Seven: Presentations and Simulations

If you wanted to see how someone would perform in an Olympic hurdles competition, a great way to see their performance would be to line them up at the starting line, pull the trigger, and check the stopwatch.

One of the best ways for organizations to accurately and consistently assess your capabilities is to actually observe your performance on tasks directly related to the kind of work expected in the position. This premise has spawned an entire industry within management selection: simulated work situations. This kind of assessment could be as simple as asking you to prepare a presentation based on some business opportunity. It could be as complex as a multiday simulation that involves you in a series of highly structured business meetings and dramatic interactions.

Providing the opportunity to perform a business-related task is both expensive and time-consuming for both the candidate and the organization. These activities would never be funded or supported if they did not help organizations to select the best candidates by yielding consistent and valid results. The fact is that production tasks are powerful indicators of future performance. An organization that employs these types of selection strategies is among the most sophisticated and discerning in the hiring process.

If you are given the chance to demonstrate your skills in a presentation or a simulation, the good news is that superior performance on this type of assessment can advance you in the race for selection. A consistent, successful strategy will be to anticipate, condition, and practice for the best possible result.

PRESENTATIONS

Watching a person deliver a formal presentation is a great equalizer in the selection process. Asking candidates to present on the same topic sets a level playing field regardless of years of experience, education, and previous level within an organization. Presentations capture the essence of leadership—the ability to organize, present, and deliver key messages in ways that convince, inspire, and engage. A powerful presentation can give a significant edge to your overall performance.

Presentations can range widely in the amount of structure and preparation. Some may be as general as asking you to present an overview of your style of leadership to the selection committee or to a constituency of employees. In more structured settings, you may be given specific materials about the organization in advance and asked to present an analysis or recommendation based on your findings. This analysis may be directly related to your functional area. Some examples of topics for these kinds of presentations include

- Provide an analysis based on a series of financial reports
- Develop a sales presentation on the company's products
- Present a competitive analysis of a current market
- Recommend a strategy for increased productivity

In each of these cases, the organization may provide you with a prescribed set of preparation materials or they may ask you to do your own research and put together a presentation. In either case, your presentation will be more precise and compelling if it is constructed and presented with a complete understanding of the organization's history, market position, recent challenges, and future aspirations. Building connections based on your thorough research of the organization will deliver a powerful message about your initiative and business acumen.

Begin your presentation design immediately upon receiving materials and instructions. In some cases this may be only a matter of days prior to an on-site visit; the last thing you want to do is hastily pull together some ideas on your flight out or begin building your PowerPoint deck in a hotel room the night before the big day. You will want to have your presentation fully crafted so that you can rehearse the presentation thoroughly in advance. Your comfort and poise with the materials will strongly impact your evaluation.

POWER STRATEGIES FOR EFFECTIVE INTERVIEW PRESENTATIONS

As you approach the presentation hurdle, the most important question to consider is, "What are the key objectives of this presentation from the perspective of the audience?" Answering this question definitively and concisely will give you the precise focus and direction that will keep your presentation on track. Review any questions or key points to be addressed in the presentation thoroughly before you dig into supporting materials. Write down no more than three overall objectives to be achieved as a direct outcome of your presentation. Begin your final preparation by ensuring you have addressed each of these points thoroughly.

- **Know your audience.** A sure way to miss the mark with your presentation is to assume you know who will be in the audience. If not told explicitly, ask your interview contact. Your presentation must be completely relevant and appropriate for your audience.
- **Conduct a brief stakeholder analysis.** List all the individuals or group constituencies that will attend your presentation. For each individual or group, list two or three points related to your presentation topic that will have significance for them.
- **Keep it simple.** A typical interview presentation lasts about twenty minutes, though it is not uncommon for a presentation to stretch to thirty minutes, especially if there will be a question and answer segment. A basic three-point structure including introduction, body, and summary will keep your twenty minutes well focused and sharp.
- **Determine if slides are essential.** In some cases, a PowerPoint presentation is considered the norm for interview presentations and may be necessary if you are reporting financials or graphical data. Powerful presentations can be delivered without PowerPoint. If your content does not require graphic or technical material, consider not using slides and a projector. Don't hesitate to ask for input on this decision.
- **Keep the presentation clean.** The goal of the interview presentation is to make meaningful connections and demonstrate your business insight—not to overwhelm the audience with data and analysis. Use white space, strong images, and brief, bulleted statements to make your presentation memorable and clear. If spreadsheets or detailed data is essential, provide these separately as handouts and distribute when needed. Always have your presentations proofed by someone else.

The most important part of your presentation is to know it cold. You must be thoroughly prepared to deliver the key points without looking at slides or note cards of any kind. Your objective is to make a very few, memorable, and clear impressions on your audience. The more comfortable you are with your material, the more successful you will be in your delivery.

SIMULATIONS

Business simulations consist of specific tasks that you are required to complete as evidence of your ability to deal effectively with typical business challenges. Simulations range in complexity from basic "in-basket" exercises to a series of interactions that replicate "a day in the life" of an experienced leader. All simulations ask you to take on a specific role—and sometimes even an identity—for the duration of the assessment. Competitors who approach simulations with an open, inquisitive, and positive attitude are most likely to demonstrate the best performance.

In-Basket Exercises

The concept of an in-basket exercise evolved from the days when managers actually had a stack of papers on their desks to deal with. Today, an in-basket exercise presents you with tasks that usually come to you as a series of e-mails. You are required to respond as effectively and efficiently as possible to each of these. In-basket exercises are focused on measuring key attributes of a candidate's work style. Some of the key competencies and capabilities assessed in in-basket exercises include

- Prioritization and time management of activities
- Insight into business processes and dynamics
- Providing delegation and direction
- Customer service orientation

- Organizational insight and political savvy
- Effectiveness of written communication
- Willingness to take appropriate risks

The best way to present your capabilities with an in-basket exercise is just to get in the same frame of mind as you would on any other workday and work your e-mail quickly and efficiently. Avoid the temptation to spend equal time on all the tasks and communication that are sent your way. Your ability to prioritize your responses efficiently will significantly impact your final score on the exercise.

Power Strategies for In-Basket Exercises
Here are some basic suggestions to maximize your performance on an in-basket exercise:

- **Skim every e-mail first.** One of the key objectives of an in-basket exercise is to prioritize tasks based on urgency. The most time sensitive or crisis-oriented issues need to be addressed quickly. After you have skimmed each e-mail, make sure you flag it or mark it as "unread" so that you are sure to go back to it.
- **Address critical issues thoroughly and completely.** In most cases you only have one chance to manage each e-mail. Think through your full response strategy before you start writing. Always include a follow-up or next step with a specific timeline.
- **Pay attention to how you delegate.** Many in-basket exercises include questions and need for additional information from your direct reports. Follow a style of delegation that seeks a balance between empowerment and micromanagement. Consider engaging people and directing them to available resources rather than giving them all the answers.
- **Explain your thinking.** The people who are evaluating and scoring your in-basket exercise typically have some precise criteria on which to evaluate your response. The clearer you are

about how you came to your conclusions, the easier it is for the evaluator to assess your performance accurately.

- **Keep responses concise.** Your performance will be based on quality, not quantity of work. Be sure that you stick to your key points and avoid rambling. The use of lists or bullet points can make your key messages easy to understand.

Pay attention to your time on the overall exercise. In more sophisticated in-basket exercises there may actually be new e-mail coming in during the exercise. If this takes place, your ability to change course and adapt quickly to new information is most likely being assessed.

"Day in the Life" Simulations

Some organizations will conduct elaborate simulations, which may be part of a day or two of assessments. These simulations include a number of staged interactions that capture a typical day in the life of a manager at the level being assessed by the client organization. Organizations are willing to invest in the significant cost of simulation-based assessment because there is strong evidence that performance on a simulation is predictive of future performance on the job. Simulation-based assessments are difficult to play or fake and tend to get at core attributes of leadership accurately and consistently.

The best way to prepare for simulation-based assessments is to understand how the simulations are constructed and scored so that you are mentally prepared for the experience. Here are design parameters for simulations:

- Simulations are generally constructed around a fictitious business. Depending on the complexity of the simulation, you will receive a detailed dossier on the business that may include organizational overview, product and market reports, financials, or other documentation specifically related to your functional area.

- Simulation-based assessments typically include two to four separate simulated activities, typically ranging in thirty to sixty minutes per interaction.
- Simulations are constructed to be appropriate for the level of management being assessed. The level and the kind of interactions conducted will represent typical challenges faced by a middle manager, the leader of a business unit, or an executive.
- Simulations will include face-to-face interactions with other individuals. These individuals are either professional actors, in which case your performance is typically videotaped and assessed, or the actors are themselves the assessors and will evaluate your performance.
- Simulations are based on typical business interactions and may include a meeting with your boss, direct reports, peers, or customers. There may also be presentations included in the simulation.
- Simulations are scored based on specific behaviors and competencies profiled for the level for which the simulation is designed.

Participating in a simulation-based assessment can be a challenging and stress-inducing ordeal. The experience can also be a great deal of fun and truly exhilarating depending on your mindset. The assessment will focus on the skills and capabilities that you have developed over many years of leadership experience. There is little that you can do in the short term to significantly change your management style and approach. In any case, the simulation is not a great place to try out radically new behaviors.

Candidates who demonstrate their best performance in simulations are individuals who are confident, relaxed, and highly responsive to the situations in which they are placed. Candidates who put on a persona that's not natural to them can easily get caught up in trying to be what they are "supposed" to be rather than being who they are. The most important aspect of high performance in the simulation is paying attention to the cues coming to you from the actors and the written materials.

POWER STRATEGIES FOR SIMULATIONS

There are several strategies that will lead you to demonstrating your best performance on simulations:

- **Study your materials.** Remember, all the information that you need to be successful will be presented in the simulation process. This means that you should carefully read and listen to every bit of information coming to you. Begin with a thorough review of any supporting materials given to you in advance, highlighting and making margin notes as necessary. This will help you access information quickly during the simulation.
- **Carefully read the instructions.** Listen to all instructions and descriptions of the simulation activities provided in advance or during the assessment. Most organizations and vendors who conduct simulations want their candidates to fully understand the experience before jumping into it. Supporting materials typically have a solid explanation of the process.
- **Brush up on key leadership skills.** Most simulations include some interactions that require negotiation and/or conflict management skills. It's helpful to review past training materials in these areas for strategies on which to build a response. My favorite website for this is Mindtools.com, which offers a remarkable array of brief articles on key leadership skills.
- **Be prepared for spreadsheets.** If you are being assessed for a financial, business unit leadership, or executive position, you'll most likely be assessed on some form of financial acumen. While it's not useful to cram an entire MBA finance course,

a quick review of the basics in finance, including how to read balance sheets and income statements, will be helpful

- **Stay in your role.** During the simulation you will likely be asked to take on a specific role and a fictitious name. Be consistent and enthusiastic about playing your role. Have fun with it. Being dismissive of the process or purposely stepping out of your role will not support a positive assessment.

As in any demanding activity, a good night of rest and a light breakfast will prepare you for the best performance. If you are traveling to the assessment site, get to your hotel room early the evening prior so that you have ample time for a thorough review of your materials.

ASSESSMENT CENTERS: BRINGING IT ALL TOGETHER

Some organizations will consolidate all assessment activities—including structured interviews, assessments, and simulations—in what is commonly referred to as an "assessment center." Activities at assessment centers typically last for one to two days and can be extraordinarily challenging and exhilarating experiences. The output of an assessment center experience is a carefully written report that summarizes dominant themes, strengths, and suitability of the candidate.

Most hiring organizations and assessment center vendors have an agreed policy that feedback on the assessment center results are not provided to a candidate unless they are hired. In some cases, there's an opportunity to debrief with a facilitator at the end of the day to get your general impression of the experience. Emphasize the aspects of the day that you found interesting and informative, but don't expect to get candid feedback on your performance. And by all means, don't reinforce any negative perceptions of your performance for the day.

Presentations and simulations can be challenging and stress-provoking events. These assessments are also fair and valid measures that accurately predict future, on-the-job performance. If you are a candidate who is both skilled and prepared, presentations and simulations provide a great opportunity to showcase your talents. These live performances can level the playing field by allowing candidates to be differentiated based on their skill in day-to-day business communications and leadership style—not just an impressive personal presence and interviewing skills.

Companies that make the investment in having candidates complete these kind of assessments demonstrate that they embrace a sophisticated approach to candidate selection. The investment of time and money associated with bringing candidates in and contracting with outside vendors to conduct the assessments are considerable. If you have made it to a point in the race where you are selected for this level of competition, you are most likely entering the final stretch with top runners and can expect the competition to be significant.

CHAPTER THIRTEEN
Hurdle Eight: Portfolios and Work Products

As you approach the final leg of your race, there's an additional hurdle that you can set for yourself. This hurdle may not be required by the organization, but preparing and executing it could significantly differentiate your overall performance.

Professionals in the areas of graphic arts, photography, film media, and marketing have always taken a full portfolio with them through the interview process. The work they produce has a visual component, so it's essential to demonstrate their abilities visually. It's also possible for executives outside the visual arts to develop a professional portfolio.

So what kind of materials would a CEO or a finance, operations, human resource, or sales professional include in a portfolio? The best place to look is the "results" section of your résumé. Ask yourself what brief documentation might illuminate each result?

Here are a few examples of what might be included in an executive portfolio:

- Press releases or an article related to a significant project you led
- One-page overview of the strategic plan or business plan you developed
- Brief analysis of the target company's competitive market
- White paper or business brief you have published
- Excerpt from a professional association presentation or article
- Picture or sample (if small) of a product that you influenced significantly
- Spreadsheet and chart showing financial performance over time in your area
- Gantt chart of a successful project that you led
- Summary sheet of ratings and selected comments from performance reviews (avoid using actual performance review reports as these may be considered confidential)

Having four or five examples of materials that provide direct support and evidence of compelling CAR stories, used at the proper time, can also boost your performance in an interview or informal discussion.

As you build your portfolio inventory, it's critical that you not share any proprietary or confidential information of present or past employers, especially if they are competitors with your target firm. Doing so would damage your credibility with the hiring organization. Internal reports should be free of specific references to the organization and no specific dollar amounts should be included in financials (use percentages). Bound workbooks, reports, and manuals that you developed could be shown to the interviewer, provided you explain that you cannot disclose the contents or leave proprietary materials behind.

Are You Ready for the Virtual Résumé?

Having solid documentation to back up your résumé is a great way to engage interviewers. What if your entire professional portfolio—reports, documents, presentations, and even video—were available on the web? Many job seekers have been moving in that direction, using blogging sites like WordPress.com, video captures on YouTube.com, and even dedicated, online résumé sites like VirtualCV.com. Some employers are now using virtual job profiles to attract the right candidates. Online dating meets job sourcing.

To see if this approach is a fit for you, and just as importantly, if this is a fit for your target organizations, start with VirtualCV.com. Review some of the samples in the professional and executive samples sections. You'll see opportunities for visually striking and interactive documentation coupled with click and play video. As with any approach you use to promote yourself online, remember that the quality of the production and layout will have as much impact on your brand as the content. If you choose to experiment in this direction, set up a test sample of your portfolio with "private" access permissions and get candid feedback from your professional network before you launch.

Why even consider developing professional portfolio items and bringing them to an interview? There are a few strategic advantages to setting and clearing this hurdle:

- During the interview process, verification of achievements is always in the back of the mind of interviewers. Whenever you can provide evidence that supports and illustrates your claims, take that opportunity to make the accomplishments tangible.
- If a portfolio piece supports one of your key behavioral event (CAR) responses, ending the response by reaching into your briefcase and pulling out a supporting document can

demonstrate your preparedness and initiative. Your portfolio may also come in handy during meals or informal conversations during your company visit.

- The portfolio approach is not a common or expected approach in the traditional interview, hence using this technique appropriately may differentiate your interview performance. A concrete example will be memorable and likely be discussed in a debrief meeting.

You might prepare a professional portfolio and never have an opportune moment to use it during an interview or visit. Even so, the process of preparation and the knowledge that you have additional resources you can use will increase your confidence and thoroughness in the interview process.

POWER STRATEGIES FOR BUILDING A PROFESSIONAL PORTFOLIO

- Review the job announcement carefully. Are there any related tasks or projects that you have completed successfully in past positions? Consider what brief documentation, report, or data output might support and illuminate your interview response.
- Consider key competencies that you'll address in a behavioral event interview. Consider portfolio materials that align or illustrate a particular leadership facet. Have at least two or three related competencies associated with a piece of material.
- Remember, it's not enough just to pull out a piece of documentation in the middle of an interview. It must fit with the specific opportunity and drive a short and compelling story. A golden opportunity arises if you are asked, "Of what accomplishments are you most proud or which demonstrate your strongest capabilities?"

- Have your portfolio organized in clearly labeled file folders in your briefcase. You should be able to grab a piece of material quickly, without hunting for it.
- A little of the professional portfolio approach tends to go a long way. Use only one or possibly two examples per interview, and, if possible, avoid using the same example for two different interviews. When interviewers compare notes, they may be less impressed if you use the same example repeatedly.

Professional portfolio materials can add depth and clarity to a traditional interview process. The right story, driven by compelling documentation, will clearly differentiate you from the competition.

DEVELOPING A NINETY-DAY ACTION PLAN

Another key opportunity to differentiate yourself is in being particularly well prepared to present your view of how the organization might move forward under your direction. If people are investing in you as a solution, they will likely want to hear how you see yourself in a new role.

This is especially true if they are recruiting in an area for which the organization does not have established expertise in your function, you are a functional head, or a business unit leader. It's also a good idea if the company is a start-up or lacks a centralized management structure, as these organizations depend on self-starters to drive initiatives and results.

A one-page, ninety-day plan for your position will compel you to think clearly and concisely about

- How you would link your thinking and action to key business strategies of the organization
- What information you would need to set your priorities
- What potential business drivers (growth, revenue, innovation, etc.) are central to the company strategies

- What the changing market conditions and competitive entries into your target company's space are
- Which peers and what functional areas you would need to engage to be successful
- What specific goals you would need to achieve in your first ninety days
- What resources you would need to achieve your goals

If you have created business plans in the past, this process should be no different except that you will base it only on inferences you have gleaned from your company research.

Once you have developed your ninety-day action plan, you have the option of presenting it in writing or using the plan for well-defined talking points during the interview. The challenge of presenting something in writing is that it may or may not fit with the expectations of the reader. This may be a particular challenge if you are working with a well-established, hierarchical organization or a founder who tends to have a strong control orientation. In that case you will want to present your ninety-day ideas as a "trial balloon" or talking points.

The ninety-day business plan is also a leverage point for you to understand the culture and flexibility of the organization as well as the specific management style of your potential new boss. If his or her eyes widen as you open up some possibilities for discussion, he or she may be less open to your entrepreneurial views. If the organization is going to be naturally resistant to your ideas or just wants an implementer, it might not be a strong fit for you.

Arriving at your interview with prepared materials that both illustrate and validate your accomplishments can be a powerful differentiator by making an impression on your interviewers. As a majority of interviews end with the interviewers holding only a résumé, any substantial and meaningful documentation you can share or leave behind keeps reinforcing key messages about your value. Simply keep in mind that less is more. One or two unique examples that fit the opportunity perfectly will have more impact than a deluge of paper.

CHAPTER FOURTEEN
Hurdle Nine: Managing Setbacks

It's possible that your race will move quickly. You might have a steady stream of contacts and interviews in the first months of your competition and a steady stream of offers and opportunities to sort through. If your race is more typical, however, you will have your share of rejections and setbacks along the way. Most races for selection include these experiences:

- Organizations string you along for weeks without a definite answer.
- Recruiters who were friendly and interested in you suddenly stop returning your calls and e-mail.
- After a long and arduous interview process that seemed to go exceptionally well, you discover there was an inside candidate slated for the role.
- You get an offer that seems great in terms of pay, opportunity, and location, but your gut tells you that you don't want to work for the organization.
- You experience a dry spell in your search; the phone doesn't ring and new leads stop appearing.

Hurdle nine is about courage and persistence—anticipating that the race will include challenges and may go on longer than expected. It is about working the strategies and maintaining the mindset essential to victory. Begin by considering how a successful competitor deals directly with specific setbacks and moves on to strategies for maintaining a long-term campaign.

SETBACKS: AN OPPORTUNITY FOR LEARNING

All the great hurdlers have had their share of bumps and falls. That is what has made them great. Setbacks have the potential to slow you down, discourage you, or fill you with doubt. The key to a quick recovery is framing setbacks for what they are: an opportunity to learn and to improve. You cannot learn and improve unless you are willing to understand your challenges, dig into root causes, and commit to building better approaches and skills. Every competitive athlete understands this.

In some cases, setbacks are due to circumstances beyond your control. The best response is to accept the situation, shake it off, and move on to the next opportunity as quickly as possible. In other cases, you have an opportunity to take full ownership of the outcome and choose to learn from the situation.

Setbacks can be explicit and direct:

- You are not being offered the job.
- You are not being forwarded for consideration.
- You do not meet the qualifications.

Rejection can also be subtle and indirect:

- The recruiter did not respond to your e-mail.
- That dinner conversation had some awkward moments.
- That interview left you with a knot in your stomach.

Regardless of the source, all rejections and significant setbacks in the selection process should trigger an After Action Review.

NEVER MISS AN AFTER ACTION REVIEW

The After Action Review is a standard practice in military and rescue operations. After a specific event, leaders sit down for an extended period of time and discuss three questions:

- What happened?
- Why did things happen the way they did?
- How can we do this better the next time?

All competitive hurdlers have their races videotaped for post-race review of their performance with their coach. The After Action Review is a standard approach and discipline for all competitors who strive to improve their performance. The process is not long and complicated; it just needs to be completed thoroughly and consistently for every significant setback or major success.

The power of the After Action Review goes back to our discussion of fear in the first part of this book. A setback can often trigger fear. The After Action Review drives the acknowledgment, acceptance, and action response that push fear away. By making the After Action Review a standard part of your race discipline, you will boost your resiliency and improve your form.

POWER STRATEGIES FOR AFTER ACTION REVIEWS

- The quality of the After Action Review will be driven by the quality of data collected. After every major call, interview, or interaction, take some brief notes—positives and negatives.

These notes will be invaluable as you practice After Action Reviews as part of your routine.

- Always conduct After Action Reviews immediately after an event, when you will be more likely to remember details and nuances. Do this particularly if it was negative or upsetting. Get back on that horse.
- Always write down your areas of success and areas for improvement; commit to specific actions moving forward. Having a clear plan to improve will minimize the tendency to replay things in your mind. Don't dwell—take action.
- Talk through your After Action Review with a friend or colleague. They may have helpful suggestions as well as insights that you are too close to see. Talking things through out loud and having a good laugh at a particular blunder or misstep will help you keep your perspective.
- Take a minute to review power strategies related to the hurdle. Are there additional strategies that you could apply in future interactions?

LEARNING FROM REJECTION

To be competitive, you must approach every selection process with the mindset that you will win the position. You should build up your hopes and envision yourself in the job. The fact is, however, that you may not win if another candidate was more qualified, interviewed more successfully, was seen as a better fit for the culture, or had more internal connections. Being told directly that you were not selected for a position that you really wanted can slam the brakes on your momentum.

As in any setback, you now have an opportunity to learn and to get better. Many candidates avoid asking for feedback on their selection performance because they just want to move away from the experience. In the case of an outright rejection, especially if you were a finalist, you have a great opportunity to get feedback that will improve your game.

For a finalist, rejection usually comes with a brief phone call. If it's an internal HR contact, they may be reluctant to provide much of an explanation other than telling you that another candidate was more qualified. Don't miss this opportunity to ask in the moment if there is there any specific feedback from the selection process that would be helpful to you as you continue your search. Most professionals will be pleased to share some additional information.

If the rejection is related through your external recruiter and the recruiter has an established relationship with the hiring company, he or she was likely given a full explanation as to why you were not selected. Ask your recruiter directly for any feedback shared. Some recruiters are reluctant to share bad news or they may seek to protect the confidentiality of their client organization. In this case you may need to press for additional feedback. Do not be shy.

A full interview process is a significant investment of your time and energy. It's reasonable to request additional feedback as a return for your investment. If your interview experiences went particularly well, or if you developed a strong rapport with a particular interviewer, there's a good chance they will connect with you. Don't hesitate to give them a call or send a brief e-mail as a follow-up. Thank them for their time, and ask them if you can have a fifteen-minute phone meeting to debrief. Some may say no, or ignore your invitation, but you'll never get potentially game changing information if you don't ask. Digging for feedback after a rejection can be painful. It can, however, also lead to significant insights that will appreciably improve your future performance.

MANAGING THE SPIRAL OF DESPAIR

In some cases, the race for selection goes far longer than anticipated. Unfortunately, in a changing economy and in an era of constant organizational change, it's not unusual for a mid-level manager search to last over ten months and an executive search for over a year. This situation can be further challenged by your geographic location. With search limitations around organizational type and location, the job search can stretch out. Keeping yourself focused and energized for the long haul requires discipline and tenacity.

The prolonged search holds a significant danger for you: a spiral of despair. The spiral starts slowly, feeding off a few negative experiences or a dry spell. The frustration and disappointment take their toll on networking activity, affecting your flow of opportunities.

Ned's Story: The Power of Taking a Break

Ned's bid for a VP of marketing position took off beautifully for the first three months. He built his home team and, like clockwork, networking led him to rich opportunities to interact with recruiters and source many promising leads. Ned quickly landed a series of interviews with various organizations; two of these progressed to offers. Unfortunately, each of the offers included significant barriers in terms of location, commute, and growth limitations. Ned turned these offers down.

The fourth and fifth months of Ned's race were decidedly different. Calls dwindled, network connections were not yielding new leads, and Ned felt that the geographic area of his search was being tapped out. Ned now experienced a growing sense of frustration, fearing that the great momentum he had built out of the gate was quickly diminishing.

Ned's wife recognized his frustration and wisely convinced him to take up an offer to join another couple for a six-day vacation in a time-share resort in Mexico. The price was reasonable and Ned conceded he could use a break.

By the third day of the trip, Ned had completely detached from his worries about the job search. During one of his excursions to the pool, he met the VP of finance from a related industry who shared a couple of interesting contacts and some great strategies from his own search that got Ned thinking about broadening his search parameters. Ned returned from his trip energized and with a fresh level of energy. Within a few weeks, Ned rebooted his drive and commitment to the search.

Financial pressures build and relationship tensions may rise, compounding the feelings of stress. The most destructive aspect of this stress is that it introduces the sound of fear into your voice and actions. Every hiring manager and every recruiter can hear the sound of fear, and it is a direct turn off. You can—you must—stop the spiral. The first step is to remember that slumps are common in the sports world, even among champions. Slumps can happen in the race for selection as well.

JOB SEARCH SLUMPS

All professional athletes have slumps at some point in their career. Slumps are just periods of time where performance drops consistently. Tiger Woods is renowned for his ability to find his way into slumps and then dig his way out. There's no secret to Tiger's approach to downturns in his game. He analyzes his shortcomings, he works relentlessly on improvement, and he continues to play the game. There is no better response than that to any slump you may encounter.

POWER STRATEGIES FOR OVERCOMING SLUMPS

- **Feed your pipeline.** One of the most common breakdowns in a job campaign is the failure to continue building new opportunities while actively interviewing or waiting for callbacks. Continual networking is vital to feeding the pipeline of new opportunities. Until you have a signed letter of employment, research and networking should continue to be daily tasks.
- **Don't narrow your focus.** The power of your bid for selection is determined by the richness and variety of opportunities you consider. Focusing all your efforts and hopes on one or two promising job opportunities may blind you to any that appear on the horizon.

- **Try something bold and aggressive.** As fear slips in, your brain (limbic system) kicks out signals that say, "Retreat, pull back, conserve." One of the best ways to overcome these signals is to take a direct and different action in your approach. Perhaps it's time to set a bold goal of directly contacting the CEOs of five target companies to discuss the value you could bring the company irrespective of any particular job listings.
- **Build out your other activities.** Success drives more success. As you conduct an extended job search, remember that success in your life activities, including your roles as a spouse, parent, volunteer, community leader, or friend all contribute to your sense of worth and confidence. Look for opportunities to build success in all areas of your life.
- **Review your race plan.** It's very easy in the heat and energy of the day-to-day job search to get off track from the original focus and outcomes of your original objectives. It may be useful to revisit the first part of this book and rework several of the key preparation activities. Doing so may reenergize your efforts and tap into the power of your original intent.

The bottom line is that if what you are doing currently is not yielding the results you want, it is time to try something different.

There is rarely an easy answer to address that challenge of an extended job search. If you find yourself in this predicament, it is of little value to beat yourself up or blame yourself. This will simply reinforce the downward spiral. The best advice, perspective, and encouragement will indeed increase your competitiveness. For the extended race, however, only your own perseverance, focus, and commitment will win the day. In the final equation, that is a choice that only you can make. All you need to do is to make that choice—every day.

CHAPTER FIFTEEN
Hurdle Ten: Acceptance and Negotiation

It's going to happen sooner or later. You're going to get that phone call, letter, or e-mail that announces that an organization is extending an offer to you. Sometimes the offer comes as a surprise, emerging from selection processes that did not seem ideal or from a company that has been silent for many weeks. Sometimes when it rains it pours, and you might receive multiple offers within a short time. Determining your strategy and approach to acceptance and negotiation is as important to victory as any other strategy in your race.

Acceptance and negotiation is the final hurdle. As tempting as it may be to leap with unbridled enthusiasm, this hurdle requires as much preparation, planning, and discipline as any other.

Your initial strategy is the starting point for successful decision making regarding acceptance and negotiation. No job, regardless of its compensation, benefits, and perks is ultimately going to pay off unless it fits with your ideal job expectations. Here is where your preparation work becomes so important. You'll be able to control the impulse to jump at something less than ideal because you have already established a clear vision of victory.

POWER STRATEGIES FOR RESPONDING TO OFFERS

As offers sometimes come as a surprise, it's important to be ready to receive an offer. With a prepared mindset and response protocol, you will get the key information you will need to begin your decision-making process. Here are some essential guidelines:

- **Always respond with polite enthusiasm.** You have absolutely nothing to gain by presenting yourself as aloof or casting yourself in a way that is different from how you interacted in the interview process.
- **Get clarity on the job.** Clarify all aspects of the job that may have been in question after your interview. This includes reporting structure, both upward and downward, major accountabilities, and span of control. Some organizations have been known to adjust job descriptions to fit a candidate.
- **Get the details.** Get the details of the total compensation package including: base salary; signing bonus; bonus structure; short- or long-term incentive structure; 401(k) matching; equity programs, including stocks and options; vacation; relocation expense, including months paid with outplacement and COBRA benefits; medical and health benefits, including dependent care; tuition reimbursement; perks, including car allowance, memberships, etc.

If there is something missing that is important to you, now is the time to ask.

- **Ask for the offer in writing.** Keep in mind that many companies do not offer employment contracts and that a letter of agreement may be standard protocol for making offers. If you have concerns about this, be prepared to seek legal counsel. If there seems to be any reluctance to put the offer in writing it's fair game to ask what might be the reason for a delay or reluctance.

- **Establish a timeline.** Respectfully ask when they would like to have a decision from you. If it's sooner than you would like, simply counter with a request for an extension. The standard response, "I need some time to think this over with my family" usually gets you a comfortable week after you receive the written offer.

If you have this written list on hand, you will not forget to ask important questions and will avoid the pitfall of responding to an offer you do not fully understand. At the end of the offer, the hiring organization should have a positive and expectant attitude to your response, and you should have all the information you need to evaluate the offer.

EVALUATING THE OFFER

Your evaluation of the offer is your defining moment, your approach to the final hurdle. In the excitement and anticipation of an offer, it's easy to get caught up in the moment. As with every major purchasing decision, there is a chance you may be sidetracked by emotions. Go back to the beginning of your search process. Review your ideal job description, your alignment worksheet, and your career development plan. Systematically review all the areas that you have specified as "nonnegotiables," "very important," and "nice to have."

You now have only three questions to answer:

1. What about this job completely engages and inspires me as an ideal fit for my career?
2. In what areas do I potentially need to compromise? (i.e., are there areas of the job responsibility, culture, location, or benefits that are less than ideal?)
3. What can I do to increase the fit with this job, either by adjusting my expectations or going back to the organization with a negotiated position?

If the answers to these questions are challenging, this is a great time to call in your home team for advice and perspective. Begin with the people closest to you, particularly if their lives are going to be directly impacted by the decision. Having three to five solid discussions of your opportunity with people who know and care about you and are willing to speak their minds is a great safety net.

UNDERSTAND THE COMPANY'S CAPACITY FOR NEGOTIATION

The more you understand your hiring organization's compensation structure, the better position you will be in to negotiate. Understanding where a company *can* move will help you focus your negotiation strategies on the areas that are most likely *to* move. In general, an organization's willingness to negotiate is determined by three major tendencies:

1. The larger and more traditional the company, the more structured and programmatic the approach to compensation.
2. The higher up in the company you are (e.g., executive level) the less a fixed and the more a complex compensation structure applies.
3. The higher the market value of you and the candidate pool you represent, the more leverage you have for negotiation.

These are guidelines; exceptions do occur. Given these tendencies, consider flexibility based on typical organization compensation structures:

- **Base pay:** Assuming the company has an established compensation structure, the job was posted at a pay band with low, medium, and high ranges. You can negotiate to the high end of that band, but it is unlikely that base pay will exceed the maximum without moving you to a different job level. There are various "catch up" strategies that may involve salary review at a specified time; failing base pay increase, you can ask how soon you can get to the level desired and what you will need to do to get there.

- **Sign-on bonus:** This will typically be listed in the offer. If you do not have moving expenses or if you were not represented by a search firm, you may have additional reasons to negotiate a larger sign-on bonus since the company saved a significant amount on your hire.

- **Cost-of-living increase:** This is typically fixed based on economic indicators, and there is little to negotiate here. It may be useful to determine what these increases have been in past years.

- **Merit pay:** Merit pay can be paid as yearly increases to your base or as lump sum payouts based on your individual performance. Ask what percentages are typically paid out in the merit program and what percentage of employees have received merit payouts. You will need to earn your merit based on performance, and you will need to negotiate with your new boss on what accomplishments rate top performance.

- **Bonus and incentive structures:** Bonus and incentive structures are typically set for certain levels of the organization based on some set of organizational performance criteria. Individual exceptions are unlikely to be negotiated (except in start-ups and for senior executive roles). Be sure to understand how your bonus program is structured (corporate, business unit, or team performance) and what the bonus payouts have been for at least the last three years.

- **Equity and retirement options:** Most retirement and equity option programs (stock grant and option plans) are very programmatic and don't flex much except for very senior positions. Dig into the programs and find out what conditions impact payouts, including timeline for full vestiture. If you're not familiar with the payout and time limitations of equity options, it would be prudent to do research here.

- **Relocation expenses:** In principle, you can make the case that relocation should not incur direct expense for you. This would include house hunting, temporary housing, commuting, and tax expenses for reimbursement benefits. Be sure that there is a budget for "incidentals," including family travel.

- **Tuition:** If you plan to move into general management and do not have an MBA, a new position is a prime time to negotiate a full-ride tuition. Assuming this will be an executive-MBA program, you can negotiate up to $40,000 a year or more. Count on having to make a three- to five-year commitment to the company in exchange for their investment.

- **Exit plan:** Do not be afraid to explore the potential of leaving the organization for reasons other than your performance or "cause." Organizations understand that there are risks associated with taking a position, especially if business conditions or recent history indicate risk (reorganization, downsizing, mergers, etc.). If you are concerned about risk of losing your job, get clarity on current policy and be willing to negotiate on severance terms and noncompete agreements.

Your approach to negotiation will inevitably color the way you enter the organization. Focusing on principles, keeping an open mind for options, and avoiding arrogant posturing will enable you to negotiate successfully without alienating the people with whom you will soon work.

FINDING OUT WHAT YOU'RE WORTH

Most companies have compensation guidelines and frameworks by which they set salary structure. Typically there is an overarching salary range for any given job level, which is driven by market data for the position and location. Companies get this information from large consulting companies that regularly survey organizations for their salary structures. Based on these reports the company derives a salary range (low, medium, high) for a given position.

The Internet has opened up access to salary information that approaches the accuracy and rigor of salary survey data. There are some key resources that make these data available online. Here are some free and accurate sites to consider:

- www.homefair.com (basic salary calculator)
- www.salary.com (basic salary calculator)
- www.glassdoor.com (basic salary calculator and anecdotal information)
- www.payscale.com (advanced salary calculator)

Keep in mind that your hiring organization salary data may be from a different source or directed by a different compensation philosophy, so don't expect perfect alignment with your offer.

NEGOTIATING AN OFFER

All leaders are expected to be strong negotiators. Senior managers are expected to represent the company's best interest in customer or vendor negotiations and consistently get the best terms. Why wouldn't you be expected to be a strong negotiator for your own position? The first step in negotiation is to decide that you are going accept the challenge—respectfully and professionally.

Once you receive your offer in writing, review it thoroughly. Determine what you really care about addressing before you respond to the company. Determine who you need to talk to. Most recruiters like to be the first point of contact, and many companies insist that all salary negotiations are handled thorough recruiting or HR. (I believe this is because hiring managers are less likely to stay within salary guidelines if they like a candidate.) If you want to negotiate salary, then it makes sense to get back to the recruiter.

If you have a question about your job, your assignments, span of control, reporting structure, or other aspects of your day-to-day accountabilities, call the hiring manager directly. Hiring managers are always anxious to hear from candidates and to close the deal. You can hear in their response their level of buy-in and support for you to come on board. If the response is flat, you have some good indication of the level of support you can expect getting started.

You should have clarity about the job role or assignment. If you have questions about assignments to certain committees or projects, job rotations, or international assignments, or possible future promotions, now is the time to get clarification. No manager can promise you a certain career path; this will be determined by your future performance. At the same time, you can clarify what level of performance is needed to reach these goals.

If there are gaps between your job offer and your ideal specifications, there is always an opportunity to negotiate when you respond. While salary and benefits are often the most anticipated points of negotiation, if you care about work-life balance there are a number of interesting ideas to add to the conversation:

- Number of expected nights of travel per month
- Flexible work hours
- Telecommuting
- Administrative support
- Transportation arrangements for long commutes

If you have done your due diligence in the interview process, you should have a good idea of areas in which the organization could be flexible. Receiving something that you already know to be contrary to company policy or culture is going to be a challenge. Organizations and hiring managers have walls (and in some cases, a hard wall) on what they have to offer. A solid push of negotiations is typically considered healthy. A long, drawn-out process probably means you're coming into the company with a solid strike against you.

GETTING TO YES

There are many perspectives on the art of negotiation. One of the most established and trusted sources on basic negotiation skills is *Getting to Yes* by Roger Fisher and William Ury. This time-honored classic remains on bestseller lists because it explains, simply and powerfully, the foundations of negotiation. The text offers three key principles you can apply to your job negotiations:

1. **Focus on interest, not positions.** Coming back to a company and saying, "$175,000 a year and 17 percent bonus structure, take or leave it" is a position. Once a position is set, both parties are stuck with attacking or defending the position. Beginning your work relationship with an ultimatum will not give you or the company a chance to negotiate.

2. **Discover the "interests" that define your shared point of view.** Interests are the logical conclusions that support your and the company's shared point of view. This is what got you the offer in the first place. Your value in terms of interests includes your industry experience, your ability to move into the role quickly, and the key capabilities that you have that differentiate you as a job candidate. Restating your shared interests is a good way to start the negotiation process.

3. **Work from objective criteria.** There are few things more powerful in negotiations than objective data that is independent

of either party. If you can make reference to reliable salary data or comparison of salaries in the same or a similar market, you're sharing an objective perspective rather than an opinion. (See "Finding Out What You're Worth," on p. 203.)

No one likes to be pushed around in negotiations. At the same time, this is your one moment of leverage to ask for what you want. Make a commitment to express your needs clearly, concisely, and dramatically.

MANAGING MULTIPLE OFFERS

Managing multiple offers is a wonderful challenge to have. In fact, the sign of a healthy campaign is to have lots of possibilities in the pipeline. Your competitive advantage lies in making decisions on current offers while holding on to opportunities that are in the pipeline. There is a constant tension between the immediate "sure thing" and the vision of the greener grass down the road.

It's not surprising that companies are often in the same dilemma as they choose candidates, often putting placements on hold while they source and evaluate additional candidates. It's a two-way street.

POWER STRATEGIES FOR MANAGING MULTIPLE OFFERS

There is no simple solution to managing this wonderful challenge. You need to keep your eyes open for the best deal while at the same time not alienating or instilling doubt in a potential employer:

- Companies anticipate that high-performing candidates may be looking at alternatives. In fact, this gives you a great basis of credibility and power in the selection process. Do not misuse this power by being evasive, cocky, or dismissive to any offer. It will clearly appear as immature and unprofessional and will sour your first impression if you do accept that job.

- Explain your situation to recruiting professionals or hiring managers factually and be clear about deadlines. Playing hiring companies directly against each other will likely blow up in your face.

- Treat companies with the same respect and deference with which you would like to be treated. No one likes to be considered a "backup choice," so if you need more time to consider another offer, just state the time you need.

- Use your objective criteria in your job design objectives and evaluate total compensation to ensure that your comparison of offers is even.

- At the end of the day, if the data don't line up clearly in one direction or another, follow your intuition. Your gut usually tells you the best solution in times of confusion.

Having candidates who are managing multiple offers is a common dynamic for most recruiting professionals. They are much more likely to understand, appreciate, and support a candidate who deals with them fairly, respectfully, and with timely responses.

AVOIDING BREAKDOWNS

Through the years, I have seen a number of seemingly successful selection races completed and proceeding to offer, only to have the hiring process breakdown. While breakdowns all have unique idiosyncrasies and driving forces, there are some common themes that seem to drive breakdowns. People often refer to this as the offer "unraveling." In some cases, offers start to unravel because the initial decision was not sound for either the candidate or the hiring organization. In some cases, it's due to poor or delayed communication.

The Damage Done in Accepting and then Rejecting Offers

There is a school of thought that suggests that business is business; if you accept a job offer and something better comes up, then it is fine to go with the better offer and simply tell the first hiring organization that you have other plans. This practice is not uncommon in a competitive job market. My purpose here is not to dictate business ethics, but I will point out, however, that the acceptance and rejections of an offer can have a very negative impact on you and others.

If the hiring organization had other candidates in their pipeline who were told that the position is filled, your action has directly impacted their job search and may result in a missed opportunity for someone else. The hiring company has invested a great deal of time and expense in you. In forcing them to reopen the search, you are wasting their investment and adding a new expense.

Hiring managers, executives, and external recruiters do not take this act lightly. It's a very small world. With networked communication within industries, expect that your actions will be communicated to others, which could potentially impact your reputation.

If you choose to mislead an organization that has offered you a job, make the choice with the full ramifications in mind.

POWER STRATEGIES FOR MANAGING BREAKDOWNS

- **Check for alignment around a hiring decision.** In some cases, organizations feel compelled to move forward with a hiring decision while there is still a lack of alignment among the primary decision makers. If you sense this dynamic, address it head-on in a frank conversation with your hiring manager. You don't want to accept a role where there is not strong support for your candidacy. Or, if you feel equal to that challenge, you will at least want to know what you are getting into.

- **Make your response timely.** With the passage of time, job dynamics change—the more time, the more change. Business conditions change, new candidates come into the picture, and current candidates get new opportunities. Silence or extended procrastination on the part of a candidate is rarely interpreted as a positive sign by the company. It's in your best interest to commit to a timeline and follow through on it.
- **Get your questions answered.** Lingering questions can grow into skepticism and doubt. This is your livelihood and your career. Do not hesitate to call your HR contact or your hiring manager with frank and open questions about any aspect of the position about which you are unclear. Be sure to ask all your questions in one call as repeated calls may be interpreted as positioning or lack of clarity on your part.
- **Understand the implications of legal review.** You need to make your own decision on when to consult an attorney. If the offer has a number of complexities that you do not clearly understand, legal review may be a good idea. At the same time, anticipate that legal negotiations may complicate and extend the acceptance process.
- **Be sure your family or significant others are on board.** Your ultimate decision to take on a new role has profound implications for the people with whom you share your life. Openly discuss the implications of your decision and get their commitment. More than one job offer has been scuttled because family members could not support the idea.

The bottom line is that a successful hiring decision must work for both the organization and the candidate. Being aware of the dynamics that lead to potential breakdowns makes you the driver rather than the victim of these dynamics.

ACCEPTING AN OFFER

Perhaps the easiest part of the race is graciously and appreciatively accepting an offer that meets all of your needs and expectations. If you have taken time to thoroughly review the offer and are confident that this is the right choice, make a call to the individual who extended the offer. Most hiring professionals appreciate the immediacy and personal nature of a call rather than an e-mail. Other than clarifying your start date, it's good to get the acceptance accomplished and not get into details about onboarding, relocation, or other aspects of the job on the acceptance call. There will be plenty of time for that and most companies have a prescribed process for follow up on new hires.

Both candidates and organizations are typically eager to take action once a job acceptance is reached. If an employment contract or letter of agreement is requested, get it sent by express mail within the next business day. This is your very first opportunity to demonstrate your responsiveness and attention to follow-through. There is no value in delaying the process.

Once the deal is done and you have a signed offer or contract, it's time to celebrate. In most cases a start date will take place at least a week or two after acceptance and most organizations will push back if a solid hire asks for an additional week for transition. Grab this opportunity for a brief vacation or some other meaningful activity. Starting a new position can be every bit as stressful and challenging as starting a job search. Take the opportunity to approach the next chapter of your career refreshed and relaxed.

GETTING READY FOR YOUR FIRST NINETY DAYS

As you run to the finish line in the race for selection, you are just beginning another race: to get acclimated, engaged, and plugged in to your new role. Most organizations with sophisticated selection processes also have developed great onboarding processes as well. Many others do not. In the latter case, it's essential that you put together your own ninety-day onboarding plan or be prepared to fill in when there are gaps.

In addition to learning how to fill out your expense reports and submit an IT ticket, a great ninety-day plan will include these key outcomes:

- Firm relationships with every individual in your reporting structure at least two levels down and one level above your boss.
- A clear understanding of organizational strategy, major initiatives, and alignment with your business or functional area.
- A clear immersion into the front-end of your business, including firsthand experience in communications with sales, marketing, customer service, and new product development.
- Direct observation of product or service deployment, including scheduled visits to production, distribution, or outlet facilities.
- A clear understanding of your performance goals (key performance indicators) and an approved goal plan within sixty days of your start date.

If the organization doesn't have these hurdles set up for you, this is your golden opportunity to design your next race.

APPENDIX
Top Leadership Competencies for Selection

Listed here are general descriptions of competencies that are commonly used in the assessment of job candidates for management positions. Each of these competencies is described at two levels. The mid-management level is about applying the competency in a particular functional or cross-functional initiative and focuses on influencing work directly. At the senior management level, the competency is focused by setting up the systems, processes, and people to achieve the outcome indirectly.

When preparing for a behavioral interview, it's important to make this initial distinction. If you are a mid-manager applying for senior-level position, you need to emphasize how you understand the work at a more strategic level of the organization.

TAKING ACTION (GETTING THINGS DONE)

One of the essential tasks of all leaders is accomplishing objectives, quickly and with measurable results. Organizations are looking for people who can manage a wide variety of accountabilities and influence large numbers of people to reach the goals of the organization on time and on budget. Linking action and outcomes to the core purpose of the organization is always a plus.

Mid-management: Demonstrate the ability to manage multiple projects within a functional area using strong project planning and budgeting skills, overcome setbacks and resource restrictions, provide people with clear direction, and hold individuals accountable for results with strong metrics.

Executive management: Demonstrate the ability to manage overarching organizational initiatives, manage resistance to change, execute business plans that reach the impact and financial targets set, coordinate multiple functions to achieve shared objectives, and coordinate efforts with peers.

COMMUNICATION SKILLS

Strong oral and written communication skills are standard expectations for any level of management. Communication skills explained in the context of a challenging business situation help to illustrate the power of personal communication style and effectiveness.

Mid-management: Demonstrate the ability to communicate business plans, priorities, and outcomes in a concise and effective way.

Executive management: Demonstrate the ability to engage, influence, and inspire individuals with strong oral and written communications, be able to speak publicly to large audiences, and motivate people to take action toward a common goal or purpose.

ASSERTIVENESS

This competency is often associated with a strong sense of identity and confidence in communicating messages, particularly tough messages, down through the organization. In this context, assertiveness often centers on opportunities where the key message diverges from the popular view or where bad news must be delivered in a direct, meaningful, and nonthreatening way.

Mid-management: Demonstrate the ability to communicate decisions and priorities from above in the organization in a way that is clear and firm, not shying away from controversy or complexity associated with the message.

Executive management: Demonstrate the ability to drive overarching messages about organizational strategy or major change initiative in a way that calms fears and elicits strong buy-in and support, particularly in situations that are stressful or challenging for those receiving the message, and to offer clarity and candor in meetings with peers.

CREATIVITY AND INNOVATION

Many organizations embrace the need to differentiate products and services through innovation. It's common for an organization to look to a new hire to bring in new ways of approaching markets, of differentiating their offerings in a unique way—allowing them to compete on value rather than price.

Mid-management: Demonstrate the ability to see ways of managing resources that uniquely identify new market opportunities, speed production, increase customer satisfaction, or increase quality and quantity of output.

Executive management: Demonstrate the ability to identify and implement processes and procedures to ensure that there is a consistent stream of innovative thinking flowing through the organization and to initiate new ways of looking at business strategy and markets.

MANAGING RELATIONSHIPS (INTERPERSONAL SKILLS)

Relationships are the vehicle by which most management decisions and actions are realized. Regardless of your intellectual prowess or work ethic, individuals who are perceived as prima donnas, empire builders, or potentially difficult to work with will inevitably be considered less favorably in the selection process.

Mid-management: Demonstrate the ability to work openly or effectively with boss, peers, direct reports, and other individuals within and outside a functional area and to respond to setbacks or conflict with poise and maturity.

Executive management: Demonstrate the ability to work with others, including executive business leaders, board of directors, and shareholders in a way that elicits trust and commitment; the ability to build a brand of trust and authenticity that fosters stable relationships down into the organization; and the ability to manage relationships with other competitive individuals.

COMMUNICATING THE VISION

Most organizations have taken the time to create a vision for the future. Most organizations also do a poor job of communicating that vision clearly and consistently in a way that aligns with action. Individuals with a track record here will have the upper hand.

Mid-management: Demonstrate the ability to clearly interpret overarching goals and objectives of the organization and translate them into meaningful priorities and actions within functional areas.

Executive management: Demonstrate the ability to create and communicate overarching goals and objectives of the organization in a way that inspires support and commitment.

SELF-AWARENESS AND SELF-CONTROL (EMOTIONAL MATURITY OR AWARENESS)

One of the challenging aspects of younger candidates vying for senior positions is that they sometimes come across as less "seasoned." Specific concerns focus on the ability to manage emotions, to bounce back quickly from setbacks, and on overall consistency of behavior.

Mid-management: Demonstrate the ability understand your strengths and developmental opportunities, to have an individual development plan in place, and to be able to talk consistently about how you have implemented actions to leverage strengths and address development opportunities.

Executive management: You are expected to have the confidence and self insight to manage yourself; to be self-effacing and avoid temptations to react with anger, frustration, demeaning behaviors, or arrogance; to rise above political gamesmanship based on a firm understanding of self and the principles of positive engagement.

CUSTOMER ORIENTATION

Whether defined as internal or external, all successful organizations focus on understanding and meeting the needs of the customer as a primary way to differentiate organizational performance.

Mid-management: Demonstrate the ability to understand key customer expectations and translate them into meaningful priorities and actions within a functional area and the ability to attract new or increased business by meeting customer needs.

Executive management: Demonstrate the ability to understand the strategic and long-term needs of customers and translate them into effective market and delivery strategies that meet specific needs and result in long-term and growing organization-to-organization relationships.

TEAMWORK AND COLLABORATION

While many organizations are better at advocating this competency than at practicing it consistently, collaboration is a frequently listed as a key competency required for a leadership position. An individual who projects a sense of singular ownership and drive around individual accomplishments may be seen as less than a team player.

Mid-management: Demonstrate the ability to build an integrated and high-performing team of direct reports that accomplishes more through collaboration than competition and to reach across functional and organizational boundaries to build coalitions that get things done.

Executive management: Demonstrate the ability to work effectively with other high-capability leaders, to manage conflict effectively when various business functions or constituencies are at odds, and to see and leverage natural synergies across the business.

ANALYTICAL THINKING AND PROBLEM SOLVING

Leadership effectiveness depends on the ability to understand and resolve problems quickly and efficiently by recognizing the root causes and implementing logical approaches to a sustained solution.

Mid-management: Demonstrate the ability to quickly and effectively identify sources of problems within functional areas at the root cause and the ability to engage and motivate others using specific tools or processes to create sustainable solutions.

Executive management: Demonstrate the ability to conceptualize large, multifaceted issues facing the organization and to integrate resources from a variety of perspectives to address the issue; and the ability to problem solve at the strategic level.

STRATEGIC THINKING

The ability to formulate and drive strategy across the organization is frequently assessed in behavioral interviews, particularly for senior-level leadership positions. Interviewers are typically interested in the clear connections made between competitive strategy and specific actions taken to achieve organizational alignment.

Mid-management: Demonstrate the ability to fully understand and interpret overarching organizational strategy and to plan and implement specific actions within functional areas to promote that strategy.

Executive management: Demonstrate the ability to formulate and communicate new strategy or consistently influence the implementation of strategy across the organization; the ability to analyze market data and competitive analysis; and to have success in establishing new markets, particularly international markets if relevant to the organization.

DEVELOPING PEOPLE

Organizations are typically interested in developing talent within the organization as a way of growing capability and retaining top talent.

Mid-management: Demonstrate the ability to quickly assess individual strengths and developmental opportunities, to quickly and creatively link learning interventions and critical experiences to prepare others for roles of greater accountability, and to effectively lead developmental discussions and coach direct reports.

Executive management: Demonstrate the ability to select and build a leadership team with complementary skill sets, to provide immediate and accurate feedback on performance of managers, and to support talent development systems and succession strategies to build capability across the organization.

DECISION MAKING

Effective decision making includes a balance between collection and analysis of sufficient information and making the decision on a timely basis. Strong responses to this competency include the ability to balance analytical rigor with speed.

Mid-management: Demonstrate the ability to make decisions quickly and efficiently so as to balance the need for analysis and action, and the ability to lead groups through effective decision-making processes.

Executive management: Demonstrate the ability to make command decisions with far-reaching implications for the organization, in some cases with limited or incomplete data to support that decision.

PLANNING AND PROJECT MANAGEMENT

Project management skills can be extremely important, particularly in the functional areas of operations and information technology. Strong candidates will have an explicit approach to, and process for, managing projects from inception to assessment of outcomes using predetermined metrics.

Mid-management: Demonstrate the ability to sell, plan, implement, and assess a significant project; and understand and apply basic project management principles, tools, and software when appropriate.

Executive management: Demonstrate the ability to build a compelling business case, plan, and implementation for a specific project involving multiple functions and demonstrate the effective return on investment in relevant financial terms

MOTIVATING OTHERS

Motivating others is a key attribute of any leadership position. Interview questions may focus on how a candidate was able to improve performance by better understanding of, and response to, individual and cultural differences in motivation.

Mid-management: Demonstrate the ability to understand differences in motivation among direct reports and leverage these motivations to achieve high performance.

Executive management: Demonstrate the ability to engage highly motivated individuals and manage potential dynamics of competition among highly competitive staff.

INTEGRITY AND ETHICS

Many managers and selection committees insist on adding integrity or ethical decision making as a core competency for any position. The implication of excluding this competency is the perception that ethical behavior is not central to the organization. Ethical behavior may be assessed by asking a candidate to respond to a hypothetical situation.

Mid-management: Demonstrate the ability to respond quickly and effectively to ethical dilemmas based on a solid sense of fairness and justice, and possibly touch on knowledge of legal precedents impacting a decision in which multiple constituencies are affected by the outcome.

Executive management: Demonstrate the ability to set the standard and expectations for the organization through personal brand and integrity and the ability to lead the organization through an ethical crisis with fast and thoughtful action.

FINANCIAL ANALYSIS AND DECISION MAKING

Financial analysis and decision making is often a key differentiator in the selection processes. Candidates who can describe the specific impact of business strategy and decisions in terms that are clear to the CFO will often have an edge.

Mid-management: Demonstrate the ability to articulate the process for creating and presenting a business case and return on investment calculation (e.g., capital expense justification) and to read income and balance statements and make inferences about top and bottom line performance.

Executive management: Demonstrate direct budget (profit and loss) accountability for an entire business and the ability to see broader trends in profitability and margin as impacted by competitive markets, supply efficiencies, product innovation, etc.

PROCESS IMPROVEMENT (LEAN, SIX SIGMA, TOTAL QUALITY)

Organizations with any roots in product development or manufacturing will have a strong orientation to quality and continuous improvement processes. If quality is a key component of the culture, count on being assessed on your formal experience and knowledge of quality practices, even if you are not in operations or engineering.

Mid-management: Demonstrate a strong orientation to quality systems; and specific experience in leading process improvement initiatives with clear, measurable impact on waste, rework, or parts without defect. Formal training and certification in quality systems may also be expected.

Executive management: Demonstrate the ability to create organizational alignment and support for quality and continuous improvement as a core business strategy and the ability to integrate quality principles into business processes.

Acknowledgments

I thank the many people who have contributed their time, creativity, and energy to the creation of this book. Our internal team includes the great efforts of Nathan McCord, Director of Research and Pat Finn Morris, Chief Editor.

Thanks to the many people who have openly shared their perspective, experience, and feedback on the book, including Colleen Bohn, Donald Creed, Jody Gold, Heather Denniston, Steve Schiera, Lance Brolin, Robert Meier, Chip Luman, Ron and Mary Kay Whittaker, Kevin Longe, Daniel Throw, Mike Lassen, Tom McClaughry, Harwood Ferguson, Will Pan, Greg Sipla, Jennifer Hayes, Jeff Bjork, Charles Hoag, Michael Harper, Karen Dorece, Lisa Lanz, John Schmidt, Jeff Carol, Dave Kurlan, Ted Cover, Jon White, Mike Hansen, Prakash Mahesh, and Mark Vance.

Thanks also to the talented and supportive team at Greenleaf Book Group, including Jonas Koffler, Sheila Parr, Jay Hodges, Bill Crawford, Jenn McMurray, Abby Kitten, and Justin Branch.

Thanks to my family, Katie, Chad, and Aaron, for all their love.